Online!

A Reference Guide to Using Internet Sources

2003 Update

Andrew Harnack
Eastern Kentucky University

Eugene Kleppinger
Eastern Kentucky University

Bedford/St. Martin's
Boston ◆ New York

For Bedford/St. Martin's

Executive Editor: Marilyn Moller
Developmental Editor: Talvi Laev
Production Editor: Colby Stong
Senior Production Supervisor: Dennis Conroy
Director of Marketing: Karen Melton
Art Director: Lucy Krikorian
Cover Design: Lucy Krikorian
Composition: Jan Ewing, Ewing Systems
Printing and Binding: RR Donnelley & Sons Company

President: Charles H. Christensen
Editorial Director: Joan E. Feinberg
Editor in Chief: Nancy Perry
Director of Editing, Design, and Production: Marcia Cohen
Managing Editor: Erica T. Appel

Library of Congress Catalog Card Number: 99-62176

Manufactured in the United States of America.

5 4 3
f e d c

For information, write: Bedford/St. Martin's, 75 Arlington Street, Boston, MA 02116   (617-399-4000)

ISBN: 0-312-41158-8

Acknowledgments

AltaVista screen shot. Copyright © 1999 AltaVista Company or its suppliers. All Rights Reserved. Used with permission.

Atlantic Cape Community College Online Course screens. Courtesy Atlantic Cape Community College, Mays Landing, New Jersey, 08330-2699.

Everest.mountainzone.com screen image. © 1999 The Zone Network, Inc. All Rights Reserved. Used with permission.

Icq.com screen. Copyright © 1998, 1999 ICQ, Inc. All Rights Reserved. Used with permission.

(Acknowledgments continued on page 250)

Preface

You hold in your hands the third edition of *Online!*—the bestselling pocket guide to using Internet sources. Whether you're a student, a teacher, or an online writer and researcher, you'll find answers to your Internet questions in *Online!* We've kept the coverage that made the first two editions so popular:

- Help finding, using, and evaluating Internet sources
- Models for citing and documenting Internet sources in the MLA, APA, CBE, and *Chicago* styles
- Tips for publishing on the Internet and the World Wide Web
- A plain-English glossary of Internet terms
- A directory of Internet sources in the major academic disciplines
- Our Web site at <http://www.bedfordstmartins.com/online>

This new edition has been updated thoroughly to reflect changes in the Internet and its use. We've also added material that makes the book more useful than ever for researchers working in a variety of disciplines.

New to the 2003 update

New features you'll find in this edition of *Online!* include the following:

- The very latest MLA and APA guidelines for citing Internet sources, including online subscription services

- New material on ethics and netiquette, including more coverage of acknowledging sources and avoiding plagiarism
- A new chapter on distance learning, with practical tips for succeeding as an online learner
- Guidelines for composing MLA-, APA-, *Chicago-,* and CBE-style hypertext essays, with complete sample papers accessible from the *Online!* Web site
- A handy FAQ guide inside the front cover
- Help citing online sources in other documentation styles

We have also taken care to update all Internet sources, incorporate the latest advances in technology, and recommend research and writing strategies that encourage responsible and effective use of the Internet.

In working on this edition, we have marveled at how far the field of citation has come since early 1996, when we began work on the first edition of our book. At that time we were trying to provide good answers to our students' questions about citing and documenting Internet sources. After reading everything we could find on using the Internet for research purposes and examining every documentation style sheet and manual available, we drafted a set of guidelines for citing Internet sources MLA-style and presented them at several professional conferences in Kentucky. We then published "Beyond the *MLA Handbook*: Documenting Electronic Sources on the Internet" in *Kairos: A Journal for Teaching Writing in Webbed Environments* 1.2 (1996) at <http://english.ttu .edu/kairos/1.2/inbox/mla.html>. That essay identified four areas of citation practice needing improvement and offered an MLA-style guide. Within days, our email boxes were flooded with requests for permission to reprint and distribute these guidelines. Enter Edith Kirkland, from Bedford/St. Martin's, who asked whether we would consider expanding our essay into a textbook. We would indeed—and *Online! A Reference Guide to Using Internet Sources* was born.

Since then, the Modern Language Association and the American Psychological Association have developed their own official styles for citing Internet sources. We're pleased to present the styles of these two organizations in Chapters 5 and 6. We're even more pleased to be part of an ongoing—indeed, an expanding—scholarly conversation about documentation and its important implications.

We've tried to make *Online!* the latest word on working with Internet sources—but we know that it's the latest word as of July 2001. And we know as well that it won't be long before new kinds of Internet sources emerge, bringing new questions. Take those questions to our site on the World Wide Web at <http://www.bed fordstmartins.com/online>. We hope this site, and this book, will be practical and useful—helpful harbors for all who navigate the Internet.

Acknowledgments

To all who have helped us prepare *Online!* we give our thanks and appreciation. We especially want to acknowledge the help of Mick Doherty, the editor of *Kairos*, for encouraging us to publish the initial essay, and Janice Walker, for her generous response to that essay. We gratefully salute the staff of Eastern Kentucky University's Academic Computing and Telecommunications Services, especially Margaret Lane and Melvin Alcorn, for their abundant and generous assistance along the way. We say thanks to all the students in Honors Rhetoric who have asked great questions about the Internet. We acknowledge all who created and subscribe to the Alliance for Computers and Writing for sustaining one of the world's most informative and helpful listservs. We are grateful to Cindy Tallis-Wright, MOO teacher extraordinaire at Diversity University, and to Joe Pellegrino, a superb webmaster and colleague.

For this edition, we benefited from the astute suggestions of the following reviewers, to whom we say thanks upon thanks: Peter L. Bayers, Quinnipiac College and Fairfield University; Anne Bliss, University of Colorado–Boulder; Mauri Collins, Old Dominion University; Saul Cornell, Ohio State University; John R. Ellison, Texas A&M University; Victor Paul Hitchcock, St. Louis Community College–Meramec; Scott Johnson, John Wood Community College; Claudine Keenan, Penn State Lehigh Valley; Judith Kirkpatrick, Kapiolani Community College; Richard C. Rich, Virginia Tech; Katherine E. Staples, Austin Community College; and Kevin Sumrall, Montgomery College.

Since the first edition of *Online!* we have benefited from the forward-looking, practical advice in *Wired Style: Principles of English Usage in the Digital Age* by Constance Hale and Jessie Scanlon. Before the publication of the second edition of *Wired Style*, Suzanne Oaks and Lisa Olney of Broadway Books allowed us an advance peek at the contents, and for this we thank them.

From the Bluegrass of Kentucky we bow eastward in deep gratitude to the many people at Bedford/St. Martin's who have helped us in our work. First of all, we thank Marilyn Moller and Talvi Laev, our wonderful and able editors whom we've come to know so well as friends and as the best of readers. We are grateful to Carla Samodulski for her contributions to the first edition. For their help with later stages of the current edition, and for coping graciously with an extremely tight schedule, we thank Colby Stong, project editor; Dennis Conroy, senior production supervisor; and Sandy Schechter, permissions manager.

Finally, we hug and cheer our families for their loving support and encouragement during the six years that *Online!* has been a part of our lives. To all, a thousand thanks!

Andrew Harnack
<andy.harnack@eku.edu>

Eugene Kleppinger
<gene.kleppinger@eku.edu>

Contents

Glossary

This glossary appears at the beginning of *Online!* because understanding the language of the Internet is crucial to your use of this book. This language includes technical terms, jargon, and even slang, and some of it may be quite new to you. If you have little or no experience using the Internet for research, take some time to read through the glossary now. Later, as you come across terms or concepts that need clarification, you'll find help here.

You'll encounter many of these terms again and again as you use the Internet—and as you use *Online!* To make the book easy to use, all the terms in the glossary are highlighted when they're introduced in the text; whenever you come across a highlighted word, know that you'll find it explained in the glossary.

To learn more about topics covered in the glossary, visit the *Online!* homepage at <http://www.bedfordstmartins.com/online>.

< > (angle brackets)   Angle brackets around text indicate that all the characters within the brackets must be treated as a single unit, with no spaces between parts, as in <http://www.infolink.org/glossary.htm>. By using angle brackets to frame handwritten or printed electronic information (e.g., email addresses and Web site locations), you prevent misinterpretation. Leave the angle brackets off such information when you type it into your browser's or email program's dialog box.

* (the asterisk)   Used in search expressions as a "wild-card" character to search for all words that begin with the letters you have specified. For example, searching for *mountain** will generate hits for *mountain, mountains, mountaineer, mountaineering,* and *mountaintop.*

@ (the "at" sign)   A fixture in every email address, @ separates the username from the domain name, indicating that you are "at" a particular electronic address. For example, <jhsmith@acs.eku.edu> indicates that someone, possibly Jane Smith, gets email at Academic Computing Services, which is at Eastern Kentucky University, an educational institution. See also *email* and *email address.*

. (the dot)   The period symbol, called "the dot" in online lingo, is used to separate parts of email addresses, URLs, and newsgroup names, as in <jhsmith@acs.eku.edu>, <http://www.yahoo.com>, and <alt.sci.ecology>.

/ (the forward slash)   Used to separate parts of URLs, as in <ftp://ftp.tidbits.com/pub>; not to be confused with the backward slash \ used in DOS directory paths.

> (the greater-than sign)   A symbol used in email messages to indicate text that is being quoted from a previous message. Most email programs automatically mark quoted text this way.

– (the minus sign)   A synonym for the Boolean operator NOT in many search tools; see *Boolean operator.*

+ (the plus sign)   A synonym for the Boolean operator AND in many search tools; see *Boolean operator.*

" " (quotation marks)   Used in a search expression to specify that the terms they enclose are to be treated as a phrase—that is, as a connected unit. Searching for *"I have been to the mountaintop"* provides hits where the words appear in that exact order.

account name   See *username.*

address book   Your collection of email addresses.

AND   See *Boolean operator.*

archive   A collection of computer files stored on a server. FTP sites are typical examples of archives.

article   Internet lingo for a message posted online.

ASCII   An acronym for American Standard Code for Information Interchange, ASCII is the most basic format for transferring files between different programs.

It is sometimes referred to in word-processing programs as "unformatted text."

asynchronous communication Electronic communication involving messages that are posted and received at different times. Email is an example of such delayed communication.

attachment A file, such as a spreadsheet or word-processed document, sent along with an email message.

bookmark (n.) A saved URL; an entry in a bookmark list.

bookmark (v.) To use your browser's menu to save a bookmark.

bookmark list A browser's pull-down menu or pop-up window containing links to Web sites you want to visit frequently; sometimes called a *hotlist.*

Boolean operator A word placed between the keywords in a search that specifies how the keywords are related. Two terms joined with AND are both required, two terms joined with OR are treated as alternatives, and a term preceded by NOT is excluded. Thus, in a search for *ships AND boats NOT Norwegian*, the resulting Web pages would all contain the words *ships* and *boats,* but none would contain the word *Norwegian.* Some search tools also treat NEAR as an operator, to find cases where two terms occur close together.

Boolean term See *Boolean operator*.

browser A computer program for navigating the Internet. Most browsers display graphics and formatted pages and let you click on hyperlinks to "jump" from one Web page to another. Widely used *graphic browsers* include HotJava, Microsoft Internet Explorer, NCSA Mosaic, and Netscape Navigator. A popular *text-only browser* is Lynx.

channel A virtual meeting place for groups or private IRCs, usually with a set topic of conversation.

chat See *IRC*.

click and hold To hold down a Macintosh mouse button (e.g., over a link or inside a frame) to open the context menu.

client A requester of information. As you surf the Internet, you, your computer, or your browser may be considered an Internet client.

context menu   A pop-up menu giving choices related to the cursor's position inside a window, opened by right-clicking the mouse (in Windows) or click-and-holding (on a Macintosh). Context menus often provide features not obtainable from a program's ordinary menu bar. The context menu for a hyperlink, for example, lets you save or bookmark that item without visiting it.

cookie   A short text file on your personal computer that stores information about your visit to a particular Web site. When you shop online, for example, the merchant's computer may ask your browser to record your color and size preferences in a cookie file. If you return to that site, the merchant's computer can read the cookie and "remember" you. (No other computers can read that cookie.)

cyber-   A prefix describing something that has been created electronically and is available online (e.g., a *cyberworld*, a *cybercity*, a *cyberstore*). *Cyber* can also stand alone as an adjective, especially to avoid clunky compounds: *cyber rights, cyber cowboy, cyber pipe dreams.*

cyberography   See *webliography.*

cyberspace   The Internet; more loosely, the online world.

cyberstalking   Using online resources maliciously to gather information about a victim's whereabouts and habits, or to pursue an unwanted contact.

dialog box   A window on your computer screen that prompts you to make choices or confirm a command to let a program continue, or a box into which you can type something. After you type your input, submit it by pressing the Enter key or clicking an onscreen button.

dialup access   Using your modem and personal computer to connect to the Internet; the main alternative to a *LAN* connection.

digital   Electronic; *wired.*

digital watermark   Ownership information embedded in a graphics file and used to trace unauthorized downloading and use of images.

directory   A list or collection of related computer files, sometimes called a *folder.* A directory may contain other directories, which are then called *subdirectories.*

directory path The sequence of directories and subdirectories you need to open to find a particular computer file. For example, the directory path <pub \data\history> shows that the *history* file is in the *data* subdirectory, which in turn is in the *pub* directory.

domain See *domain name*.

domain name The string of letters and symbols associated with a Web site or email service provider, as in <www.enigmacom.com>. A domain name has at least two *elements* (parts), separated by periods. The first element or elements uniquely identify an organization's server, while the final element, called the *domain*, identifies the type of organization operating the server. Common suffixes include *.com* (commercial), *.edu* (educational), *.gov* (government), *.mil* (military), *.net* (network management), and *.org* (noncommercial/nonprofit). Domain names sometimes identify the country in which a server is located (e.g., *.au* for Australia, *.ch* for Switzerland).

download To transfer information electronically from one computer to another, as when you move a program from an archive to your computer.

driver Software used by your computer system to control a printer, scanner, or other device.

ejournal (electronic journal) A journal, popular or scholarly, published primarily on the Internet.

email (electronic mail) Any of various programs that send and receive messages over a network.

email address The address you use to send and receive email. Your email address contains your username, the @ symbol, and the domain name, as in <jhsmith@acs.eku.edu>.

emoticons Small graphic renderings, composed of ASCII characters, that writers substitute for facial expressions and body language. Emoticons are useful in an online world where curt or hastily written messages can easily offend, and where you may want to indicate humor, surprise, or some other emotion to readers who cannot see you. Some of the most popular emoticons are :-) (smile), :-((frown), :-/ (skeptical), }:-> (devilish), and :-o (surprised). For a fuller list, see *Internet Smileys* a <http://www.smileydictionary.com>.

extension   The letters following the dot in a filename. Common extensions for Web files include *.gif, .htm, .html, .jpg, .mov,* and *.wav.*

ezine (electronic magazine)   A magazine published primarily on the Internet

FAQ (frequently asked questions)   Pronounced "eff-ay-cue" or "fack"; a file containing answers to common questions that new users of a program or service might ask. If you are new to a newsgroup or listserv, look up the group's FAQ file and read the answers to questions others have already asked.

favorite   A bookmark in Microsoft Internet Explorer. See also *bookmark (n.).*

flame (n.)   A personal attack on someone, usually within a listserv or newsgroup thread.

flame (v.)   To send a *flame (n.),* as in "She *flamed* me."

frame   A distinct part of a Web page, with its own scroll bars. Links in one frame often control the display in other frames on the same page.

freeware   Software that you can download and use on your personal computer without charge.

FTP (file transfer protocol)   The set of commands used to transfer files between computers on the Internet.

GIF (graphics interchange format)   Pronounced "jiff" or "giff"; one of two common formats (the other is JPEG) for image files associated with Web documents. The acronym appears at the end of the filename, as in <everest.gif>.

gopher   A program for accessing Internet information through hierarchical menus, gopher will "go for" the information you select and will display it on your screen. Gopher's text-oriented file format makes it especially useful for searching large collections of texts such as electronic books, library catalogs, historical documents, and specialized databases. On the World Wide Web, gopher addresses begin with *gopher://* instead of *http://*.

graphic browser   A program on your personal computer that finds and displays Web pages. The most popular graphic browsers are Microsoft Internet Explorer and Netscape Communicator.

graphic interface A set of computer controls designed to let the user interact with the operating system pictorially—that is, by using a mouse to select from menus, icons, and images, rather than strictly through keyboard typing.

header The area in an email message that contains routing information—who sent the message, where the message originated, the date it was sent, the route it took, and so on.

history list A list (usually a pull-down menu) of the Web pages you most recently visited. History lists let you return quickly to a site or see an overview of your latest surfing session.

hit In Internet lingo, hit can mean (1) an item in the list of search results a browser gives you ("AltaVista's search for *scorpions* turned up sixty-nine hits"), or (2) accessing of a Web page by an Internet surfer ("The *Online!* Web page received three dozen hits this week").

homepage Usually the first page you see when you access a particular Web site, a homepage has hypertext links to other pages on the same server or to other Web servers.

hotlink See *hyperlink*.

hotlist See *bookmark list*.

HTML (hypertext markup language) A computer code that allows you to create pages on the World Wide Web. HTML "tags" electronic text to indicate how it should be displayed onscreen by browsers. It provides a common language for browsers using different computer systems (Mac, PC, Unix, etc.).

HTTP (hypertext transfer protocol) The communication rules used by browsers and servers to move HTML documents across the Web.

hyperfiction Fiction composed as hypertext.

hyperlink A connection between two places on the Web. Hyperlinks are represented onscreen by highlighted icons or text. Selecting a hyperlink makes your browser "jump" from one place to another. Hyperlinks are sometimes called *hotlinks*.

hypertext A document coded in HTML; a collection of such documents.

hypertext link A connection between two documents or sections of a document on the Web; a type of *hyperlink*.

hypertext markup language   See *HTML.*

hypertext transfer protocol   See *HTTP.*

ICQ   An Internet chat program, named for the words "I Seek You."

image map   An image containing clickable links to other Web documents.

instant messaging   See *IRC.*

interface   The set of buttons, keys, menus, and commands available to control computer operations. See also *graphic interface.*

Internet   A vast network of computers offering many types of services, including email and access to the World Wide Web. As a "network of networks," the Internet links computers around the world.

IP (Internet protocol) number   A four-segment number, such as 157.89.104.11, that uniquely identifies a particular computer connected to the Internet. Your Internet service provider may specify which number you must use, or your computer may obtain its IP number automatically whenever you connect to the network.

Internet relay chat   See *IRC.*

Internet service provider (ISP)   A person or company providing access to the Internet.

IRC (Internet relay chat)   The online equivalent of CB radio and telephone conferencing, IRC lets you communicate synchronously (in "real time") with other people. See also *real-time communication.*

ISP   See *Internet service provider.*

JPEG (Joint Photographic Experts Group)   Pronounced "jay-peg"; one of two common formats (the other is GIF) for image files associated with Web documents. In filenames the acronym appears as *jpeg* or *jpg,* as in <pluto.jpg>.

keyword   The term you type into a search tool's dialog box; what you want to search for.

LAN (local area network)   A set of computers connected in order to communicate and share resources within a limited geographic area (e.g., an office building).

listowner   The person responsible for maintaining and/or monitoring a listserv.

listserv   An ongoing email discussion about a technical or nontechnical issue. Participants subscribe via a central service, and listservs may have a moderator who manages information flow and content. (LIST-SERV is software licensed by L-Soft International, Inc., for management of electronic mailing lists. Similar products include ListProc, from the Corporation for Research and Educational Marketing, and Majordomo, distributed through <http://www.greatcircle .com>.)

local area network   See *LAN.*

location bar   The space in which a browser reports the URL for the current page, and into which a computer user types a desired page's URL.

logical operator   A word that defines how another term should be treated in a search request. See *Boolean operator.*

lurk   To watch or read without participating. Lurking on a listserv, for example, means that you read other people's messages but don't post messages yourself.

metasearch engine   See *metaengine.*

metaengine   A Web search tool that combines results from several independent searches.

modem   Equipment that connects a computer to a data transmission line (usually a telephone line), enabling the computer to communicate with other computers and the Internet.

moderator   The person who reads all messages sent to a moderated newsgroup and decides whether a particular message is appropriate for posting.

MOO (multi-user domain, object-oriented)   An electronic "space" in which many people can interact simultaneously. Accessible through telnet, MOOs enable classes, seminars, and friends to meet at a given time, usually to discuss a given topic.

MUD (multi-user domain)   As electronic "spaces" for simultaneous communication, MUDs provide opportunities for role-playing in which each participant usually controls one character who has a complete life history and persona and can express a variety of physical and emotional responses.

NEAR   See *Boolean operator.*

netiquette A combination of the words *Net* and *etiquette, netiquette* refers to appropriate behavior on a network, and specifically on the Internet.

netizen Any person using the Internet.

newbie Someone new to the Internet; a beginner.

newsgroup A group of people and their collection of postings on the Usenet network. Newsgroups are open forums in which anyone may participate. Each newsgroup has a topic, which can be as broad as the focus of <alt.activism> or as narrow as the computer applications discusssed in <comp.sys.mac.apps>. See also *Usenet.*

NOT See *Boolean operator.*

online On a network; on the Internet.

OR See *Boolean operator.*

password A personal code you use to access your computer account and keep it private.

PDF (portable document format) A file format that provides a graphic image of a printed page, suitable for viewing and printing, and usable on many different operating systems. PDF documents are easily viewed through Adobe Acrobat Reader, which can be downloaded at no charge from Adobe at <http://www.adobe.com>.

pixel Shorthand for *picture element;* the smallest visible colored or monochrome dot a computer monitor can display.

plug-in Add-on software to increase a browser's capabilities.

portal A gateway or starting site for Web exploration. Users frequently point their browsers to well-known portals such as Netscape Netcenter <http://home.netscape.com> or Yahoo! <http://www.yahoo.com>.

post To send a message to someone online.

posting An online message.

protocol A set of commands—the "language"—that computers use to exchange information. Often-used protocols include FTP, gopher, HTTP, mailto, and telnet.

real-time communication Electronic communication in which people converse simultaneously with one another; also called *synchronous communication.* MOOs,

MUDs, IRCs, and ICQ are examples of real-time communication.

right-click To use the right-side mouse button in Windows to open the context menu, which contains special functions for saving files and bookmarking. In Macintosh systems, you click and hold to open the context menu.

search engine See *search tool*.

search tool Any of various programs that work with your browser to find information on the Web. After you type a keyword or keywords into your browser's dialog box, a search tool looks for Web pages containing your keyword(s) and produces a menu of available documents (hits). Also called *search engine*.

server A computer or program that handles requests from client computers for data, email, file transfer, and other network services.

shareware Software that you can download and use on your personal computer according to the conditions specified by the provider. Typically, you must pay a small fee in order to keep using a shareware program after you have tried it.

signature (sig) file A text and/or graphics file appended to your email and other postings. Signature files generally contain a name, an offline contact address, and sometimes a quotation or pithy saying.

snailmail (n.) The U.S. Postal Service or another agency that delivers messages by courier.

snailmail (v.) To use snailmail.

spam (n.) Unwanted email (e.g., junk mail).

spam (v.) To fill someone's email with *spam (n.)*.

status bar The text and icons at the bottom of a browser window that keep you informed about the progress of a connection or the location of a link you have selected (before you click it).

subject directory A Web site that categorizes many other Web sites by topic. Yahoo! and Refdesk are popular subject directories.

subject guide See *webliography*.

subject line The title of a message as it appears in an email, listerv, or Web discussion forum menu.

surf To navigate the Internet. A *surfer* is an avid Internet user.

syllaweb   Online syllabus.

synchronous communication   See *real-time communica-tion.*

TCP/IP   An abbreviation for *transmission control proto-col/Internet protocol,* TCP/IP controls software appli-cations on the Internet.

teleport   To "transport" a person or object electronical-ly across a virtual space. In MOOs, characters and objects can be teleported instantaneously from one location to another.

telnet (n.)   A program that lets you log onto another computer from your own computer using a user-name and a password.

telnet (v.)   To use telnet.

terminal connection   A way to join computers, using modems or a network, that allows only text trans-missions. Although they are not suitable for graphic browsing, terminal connections are still used with a few email programs and with many library catalogs.

text index   A Web site that indexes the words on mil-lions of Web pages and lets you search for pages con-taining the keywords you specify. AltaVista and Hot-Bot are popular text indexes.

thread   A series of postings about a particular topic. For example, you might decide to follow a *fire ants* thread in the newsgroup <alt.sci.ecology>.

thumbnail   A miniature rendering of an image; used on the Web as a link to the full-sized version.

toggle   To turn on and off, as a light switch.

URL (uniform resource locator)   Pronounced "you-are-ell." A string of characters that uniquely identifies each page of information on the World Wide Web; a Web address. The URL for *Online!* is <http://www.bedfordstmartins.com/online>.

Usenet   A network providing access to electronic dis-cussion groups (newsgroups). You can join any of thousands of Usenet newsgroups by using a news-reader program.

Usenet newsgroup   See *newsgroup.*

username   The information that, combined with your password, lets you access your computer account; also called *account name, charactername, userid.* Your

Internet email address probably begins with your username.

virtual   Online; occurring or existing in cyberspace.

virus   A computer program designed to act maliciously on other computers. Viruses are so named because they spread quickly between systems and across networks when infected programs, data files, or storage media (e.g., floppy disks) are shared.

Web   See *World Wide Web*.

Web browser   See *browser*.

Web discussion forum   A Web page offering articles to read and giving readers special tools for responding online to articles and responses already posted by others. In a typical discussion forum, all contributions are automatically added to the Web page, whose topically arranged menu gives convenient access to *threads* (ongoing discussions on specific topics).

Web page   A hypertext file, and other files associated with it, that a graphic browser displays as a single unit in a window on your computer. *Web page* is also used synonymously with *URL,* as in "What's your Web page?"

Web site   Any location on the World Wide Web.

webfolio   A collection of a student's texts published for review on the Web. Writing instructors teaching online often ask students to submit webfolios instead of printed portfolios. Businesses, craftspeople, and artists create webfolios to display their products, services, and artwork.

webliography   (1) An electronic bibliography (also called a *cyberography*); (2) a Web site linking many Internet resources for a specific topic (also called a *subject guide*).

wired   Electronic; online.

wizard   (1) An administrator of a MOO; (2) a feature included in some programs that provides step-by-step guidance to help users perform tasks.

World Wide Web (WWW)   A global Internet service connecting hypertext data and resources. Using a browser, you can move quickly from one Web site to another in search of information, graphics, and data.

To find out more about Internet terms, visit the *Online!* Web site or consult the following resources:

ILC Glossary of Internet Terms
<http://www.matisse.net/files/glossary.html>

Netdictionary
<http://www.netdictionary.com>

Whatis.com
<http://whatis.com>

Wired Style
<wiredstyle@wired.com>

CHAPTER ONE

Finding Internet Sources

Have you been to the summit of Mount Everest? Have you wondered what's it like to be at the South Pole? Would you like to take an armchair tour of a distant country before visiting it in person or preparing a report about its culture? All of these experiences are at your fingertips through the communications system called the **Internet**, which brings the sights and sounds of places around the globe to your personal computer.

Visiting a distant place via the Internet is not quite the same as being there in person, of course. But **virtual** explorations do let you "travel" anytime you like (regardless of time of day, weather, passport restrictions, or your personal health), and you can linger and look around as long as you wish. Best of all, your trip is inexpensive (perhaps free!), and you stay safe and comfortable right where you are, with no chance of dropping your camera or losing your luggage.

To find out what an Internet exploration is like, you can visit the Mountain Zone Everest **World Wide Web site** at <http://www.everest.mountainzone.com> and see the archives of an entire expedition, from the base camp to the summit and back, with photographs, video clips, and audio descriptions of the climb (see Figure 1.1). Other links from this homepage offer live video feeds from current Everest climbs, pages of interesting facts about the Himalayas, and archives of weather data collected on the mountain. You can even ask questions of Everest explorers and read comments posted by others, or download an Everest screen saver for your computer desktop.

To explore other destinations around the world, visit these sites:

National Geographic <http://www
.nationalgeographic.com>

NOVA <http://www.pbs.org/nova>

Figure 1.1
A view of Mount Everest
<http://everest.mountainzone.com/99/south/photos/classic
/top-7.jpg>

Visiting faraway locations via the Web is not only entertaining but academically useful. In the course of your trip to Mount Everest, for example, you might become interested in the legends surrounding the landmark, or in learning safety precautions for high-altitude mountain climbing. Throughout *Online!* you'll see how themes like these can successfully be developed into essays that include Internet sources.

Finding information on the Internet brings new opportunities—and new challenges. The Internet is *democratic:* all voices have an equal chance to be heard. The Internet is *global:* you can read an online document published anywhere in the world. The Internet is *up-to-the-minute:* facts and figures can be as fresh as the second you request them. The Internet is *interactive,* promoting communication as intimate as personal **email** and as public as online journals and Internet conferencing. Best of all, the Internet is *free:* the information found there typically costs absolutely nothing. (You may have to pay for access to the Internet, but most of the files you find are free.)

Because Internet publishing is at once democratic, inexpensive, global, and instantaneous (and because it often bypasses the formalities of print publishing), you need to be concerned about the reliability of what you discover there. Helping you evaluate the reliability of Internet sources is one of the goals of this book. (See Chapter 4.)

1a Understanding the Internet

The **Internet**—sometimes simply called the Net—links computers around the world. When you're connected to the Internet, you can communicate with people, schools, organizations, governments, businesses—anyone who has a computer with an Internet connection. In **cyberspace**—the electronic world you go to when you communicate with others by computer—you can listen to distant radio broadcasts, watch movie clips, play chess around the clock with someone in Russia, send email to a friend in South America, chat with colleagues every Tuesday evening, do research on any topic imaginable, contact manufacturers' hotlines—even shop for a used car.

So when you think of the Internet, think big. Imagine the Net as the communications mall of the world, a place

Box 1.1
The Internet's information sources

Here's what you'll find when you use the following sources:

World Wide Web   texts, graphics, sounds, videos on every topic imaginable

email   personal messages and attached files

Web discussion forums   Web pages holding articles, ideas, questions, and comments addressed to specific audiences and posted for public discussion

listservs   email messages on specific topics, exchanged between subscribers

newsgroups   email-like bulletin boards storing messages addressed to specific communities of Internet users and posted for public discussion

real-time communication   electronic forums or "rooms" for conversing with others and attending online classes and conferences

FTP, gopher, telnet   files, texts, and connections to other computers

where millions of people can communicate with one another. Like all large malls, the Internet has numerous entrances, information centers, levels, concourses, and specialized areas. Box 1.1 shows some of the *cyberplaces*—the virtual gatherings, events, information sites, and services—you can currently explore on the Internet.

1b   Connecting to the Internet

Getting on the Internet is not difficult. All you need are a computer, a modem, and browsing software. A **modem** connects a computer to a phone line or a cable television line; a **browser** helps you find places on the Internet. While individual computers may differ in how they are connected to the Internet, nearly all Internet connections provide the same basic services. Your **Internet service provider (ISP)**—perhaps your school's computer center, your telephone or cable company, a government or nonprofit organization, or a local or national commercial service such as Prodigy or America Online—connects your computer to the Internet.

If you're connecting to the Internet from your home or apartment, enlist the services of an ISP. Your ISP will assign you a **username** (sometimes called an *account name* or a *userid*) and a **password**. Get the name and telephone number of a contact person to call at your ISP in case you have trouble connecting (e.g., if your password no longer works). Keep your ISP account information in a safe place. If you suspect your own computer is the source of your trouble, consult a computer technician.

If you're working with your own Internet connection, you can find help in Internet access guides, such as *The Complete Idiot's Guide to the Internet,* published by Que Corporation, or *The Internet for Dummies,* published by IDG Books Worldwide. All the Internet software you need will be provided by your ISP, or you can download it from TUCOWS at <http://www.tucows.com>. When you've made your Internet connection, go to Chapter 2 of *Online!* for tips on accessing specific Internet sources.

To learn more about the Internet, its history, how it works, or emerging Internet technologies, visit the following **Web sites**:

A Brief History of the Internet (*Walt Howe*)
<http://www.walthowe.com/navnet/history.html>

NUA Internet Surveys
<http://www.nua.ie/surveys>

NUA Internet Surveys tracks use of the Internet for business, social, and technical purposes and publishes a weekly newsletter analyzing current trends.

1c Navigating the Internet's World Wide Web

When you go to the **World Wide Web**, you enter a world of **hypertext** connections linking millions of electronic sites. Your computer communicates with such **Web sites** by following a set of basic rules called **TCP/IP (transmission control protocol/Internet protocol)** that provide a common language usable by all computer operating systems. **Browsers**—software programs that translate your keyboard-and-mouse activities into TCP/IP—find the multimedia information you seek and display it on your screen. (Popular browsers include Netscape Communicator and Microsoft Internet Explorer.) When your computer retrieves information for you, it acts as a **client** working with **servers** (other computers).

Nearly all of the information available on the Web is published in **Web pages** composed of **hypertext**. Written in **HTML (hypertext markup language)**, Web pages contain **hypertext links**—usually represented by highlighted words or pictures—that alert you to the easy availability of more information. The links in a document may point to other portions of the same document, to other documents at the same location, or to any other document anywhere on the Internet. The hypertexts and their links form a three-dimensional electronic "web."

1d Understanding URLs

Every hypertext link contains a **URL (uniform resource locator)** that points to a specific Web site. Most URLs represent the address of a computer file or **directory** (collection of files).

1 Dissecting URLs

Here is how a typical URL looks:

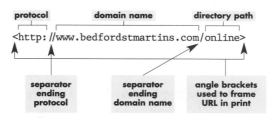

While some Internet humorists would have you believe that the abbreviation **HTTP** means "head to this point," it actually stands for **hypertext transfer protocol**. In a URL, the prefix *http:* represents the **protocol** (kind of link to be made). The two **forward slashes** after the colon show that the link will be to another computer. (URLs use forward slashes, never the backward slashes used in DOS directory paths.) The **domain name** identifies the owner of the Web site (in this case, Bedford/St. Martin's);

the last part of the domain name, *.com,* shows that the owner is a commercial entity. A slash separates the domain name from the **directory path**, which is the "address" of the part of the Web site that this particular URL leads to. **Angle brackets** separate the URL from surrounding text.

URLs for World Wide Web sites always begin with *http://.* Other frequently used Internet protocols and their prefixes include **FTP** *(ftp://),* **gopher** *(gopher://),* news *(news://),* **telnet** *(telnet://),* and the mail protocol *mailto:* (which does not use slashes). URLs for these protocols follow the *http://*pattern but often include other elements such as an **email address** or a **newsgroup** name.

When you click on an onscreen link, your browser uses the associated URL to retrieve the information and display it on your computer. Every browser also includes a **dialog box** or **location bar** where you can enter a URL; pressing the Enter key sends your browser into action. Furthermore, you can use your browser's **bookmark** feature to record the URL and, later, to return quickly to the same page.

For more help with finding and using URLs, see 1d-2 and 1d-3.

To learn more about the technical details of URLs, consult the Web document *Naming and Addressing, URIs, URLs, URNs, URCs* at <http://www.w3.org/Addressing>.

2 Typing URLs

Take care when typing a URL because every letter, symbol, and punctuation mark is significant for computer communication; any extra or missing marks or spaces will prevent you from making a successful link. Always reproduce capitalization accurately. When showing URLs as part of text you're writing, enclose each URL in **angle brackets—< >**—for two reasons:

1. Enclosing a URL in angle brackets tells readers that everything within the brackets is part of the URL (even if the printed text breaks the URL in the middle so that it appears on two lines).
2. Bracketing a URL lets you use punctuation around the URL without introducing ambiguity about whether the punctuation is part of the URL.

The following sentence shows how angle brackets clarify where a URL begins and ends:

▶ For clear answers to questions about grammar, style, and usage, visit the Purdue On-Line Writing Laboratory at <http://owl.english .purdue.edu>; you'll especially enjoy its linked advice on punctuation at <http://owl.english .purdue.edu/handouts/grammar/index.html>.

URLs can be extremely long, running to hundreds of characters. In printed text, a long URL must often be divided. The following rules for breaking URLs are adapted from *Wired Style* (Broadway Books, 1999), by Constance Hale and Jessie Scanlon.[1]

- *Break a URL after the protocol abbreviation that begins it—http:// , gopher:// , ftp://;* don't break the abbreviation.

- *Break a URL before a punctuation mark,* moving the punctuation mark to the following line. (The following symbols function as punctuation marks in URLs: tilde ~, hyphen -, underscore _, period or dot ., forward slash /, backslash \, pipe |.)

- *As a last resort, break a URL in the middle of a word,* where you would normally hyphenate the word (but don't hyphenate the break).

Here are examples of acceptable breaks for URLs:

▶ <gopher://
gopher.tc.umn.edu:70/11/Libraries/Electronic
%20Books>

▶ <http://www.cc.gatech.edu/fac/Amy.Bruckman
/moose-crossing>

▶ <http://www.w3.org/pub/WWW/Address
ing/Addressing.html>

Finally, when you enter a URL into your browser's dialog box, remember to type everything *except the angle brackets.*

---

[1]The *MLA Handbook for Writers of Research Papers* (New York: Modern Language Association, 2003) recommends slightly different rules for line breaks, and our model citations reflect those differences. (See Chapters 5–8.)

3 What to do when a URL doesn't work

When typing a URL into your browser's dialog box produces an error message such as "File not found" or "Host
not found," don't give up! Instead, try the following
tricks:

1. If you typed the URL, check every letter and character for accuracy. If you copied a hyphen from the end
   of a printed line, try deleting it.
2. Delete any spaces, quotation marks, or angle brackets, and change all commas to periods. Make sure all
   periods are single (.), not multiple (..). Make sure
   there is no period at the end of the URL.
3. Use only forward slashes (/).
4. Look for simple mistakes in URLs or file names
   (e.g., misspelled words or abbreviations). For example, the URL <http://wwww.uhawaii.edy> contains
   two errors and can easily be changed to <http://www
   .uhawaii.edu>, which will work. (Errors frequently
   appear at the ends of URLs; most Web file names end
   with the **extension** *.asp, .htm, .html, .gif, .jpg, .txt, .wav,*
   or *.mov*.)
5. Change uppercase letters to lowercase ones; change
   the numerals 1 and 0 to the letters l and o.
6. At the end of the URL, try substituting *.htm* for *.html*
   and vice versa.
7. Try backstepping: delete the last element in the URL
   (up to a slash), and then press Enter. If you succeed
   this time, inspect the file carefully to see whether it
   contains a link to the information you were seeking.
   (The file you want might have been moved.) You can
   continue backstepping all the way to the **domain
   name** (and you might find a Search function along
   the way that will help you find the document!).
       Here's an example of a backstepping sequence:
       <http://www.exam.com/~home/people/welcome
       .html>
       <http://www.exam.com/~home/people>
       <http://www.exam.com/~home>
       <http://www.exam.com>
8. On the pages you see while backstepping, look for
   the email addresses of people you might contact
   about the missing file.

1e Narrowing a general topic

You can use the Internet to narrow a general topic to a more specific topic you want to research. Suppose you're interested in researching adoption. The Internet is rapidly becoming *the* major clearinghouse for adoption information because it connects people with sources on all aspects of adoption issues and permits quick exchange of information. **Surfing** Internet discussions of child adoption, you'll find a wide range of information, from scholarly expertise to personal pleas for help. One of the greatest achievements of the Internet is that it lets everyone's electronic voice be heard.

A preliminary Internet search on child adoption reveals many possible subtopics:

Searching for one's biological parents or children

Searching for prospective adoptive parents or children

Learning how to evaluate the health of available adoptees

Finding sources of support for adoptive families

Reading and analyzing stories about adoption

Working to improve adoption law

Each item on this list represents vast amounts of electronically published materials available in many forms. The main difficulty is not so much knowing where to begin—you could just go to the library and look up *adoption*—but knowing how to narrow your focus quickly, to browse through sources comprehensively yet efficiently. Although some very important resources such as legal databases and hospital birth records are not yet Internet-connected and must be accessed in more traditional ways, many adoption organizations provide Internet help in using such services. Internet tools for surveying and narrowing a topic are described in 1g-1.

1f Researching a specific topic

Sometimes you'll start your research with a fairly specific topic in mind. Suppose you want to know more about Charlotte Perkins Gilman's "The Yellow Wallpaper," a short story published in 1892 that recounts a woman's descent into depression and (perhaps) insanity as she

struggles to express herself within her husband's ago-
nizing restrictions. Because of its feminist elements and
its powerful description of depression, the story appears
regularly on reading lists for courses in literature, psychology, and women's studies. If you do an Internet text
search for the **keywords** *yellow wallpaper*, you'll retrieve
hundreds of **hits** (items matching your request), including many Web pages for classes where the story is being
discussed. Among these pages is The *Yellow Wallpaper*
Site at <http://www.cwrl.utexas.edu/~daniel/amlit
/wallpaper/wallpaper.html>, created to accompany an
American literature course and maintained as an ongoing Web project. Through this page you can read an
online edition of the story, find historical details about
the author and the story's publication, read critics' comments and students' essays, select related Internet links,
and even contribute to the ongoing discussion. If you
leave a comment or ask a question, perhaps about the
story's puzzling ending, your message automatically
appears within the forum, and others can then reply to
you the same way.

To see what other literary works are being explored
similarly, visit the American Literature Survey Site at
<http://www.cwrl.utexas.edu/~daniel/amlit/amlit
.htm> or search the Internet for the phrase *interactive
texts*. For example, at <http://www.cwrl.utexas.edu
/~daniel/amlit/bartleby/bartleby.html> you can read
not only Herman Melville's "Bartleby the Scrivener" but
also student essays about the work, and you can add
your own comments.

1g-2 describes Internet tools for researching a specific
topic.

1g   Searching with Internet tools

You can use many different programs to search for information. Selecting the most efficient **search tool (search
engine)** for a particular topic usually means choosing
between two kinds of tools: those providing **subject
directories** and those listing **text indexes**.

Subject directories work like telephone book yellow
pages, listing Web sites by predetermined categories.
You select a category by clicking the headings on the
directory's homepage, or use the directory's search function to find categories that contain the term you're inter-

ested in. Then the directory shows you any relevant sub-categories and sites. When you click on a site's link, you leave the directory's menus and visit that page. You can then return to the directory's page with your browser's Back button.

Text indexes let you scan documents for specific terms. The indexing service uses robot programs that periodically comb through the Internet, recording each occurrence of every word or phrase found. When you enter a search term, the index returns a list of sites that contained your term when the robot last cataloged them. Search results differ from one index to another, mostly because of variations in scope and frequency of cataloging.

When you want to see what the Internet offers about a broad topic, use a subject directory; when you want to see which Internet sites contain a particular word or phrase, use a text index.

New Internet search tools appear almost every month, and existing search tools are continually being improved. As you encounter new or revised tools, be sure to check their Help documents for the latest developments and search hints. For up-to-date information about search tools, consult the Yahoo! menu at <http://dir.yahoo.com/Computers_and_Internet/internet/world _wide_web/searching_the_web>.

1 Subject directories

Suppose you know the broad topic you want to research, but you haven't yet chosen a narrower subtopic to focus on. For example, you might be interested in Mount Everest but not know what subtopics are available for exploration. To find out, you could use one or more of the search tools listed in Box 1.2. All these tools index the World Wide Web's contents by subject category and offer the results in a subject directory. This section describes some of the most useful subject-directory search tools.

INFOMINE
<http://infomine.ecr.edu>

INFOMINE specializes in organizing a large set of "scholarly Internet resource collections." From the **homepage**,

Box 1.2
Some popular subject-directory search tools

INFOMINE <http://infomine.ucr.edu>
The Internet Public Library <http://www.ipl.org>
Librarian's Index to the Internet <http://lii.org>
Library of Congress Home Page <http://lcweb.loc.gov>
LookSmart <http://www.looksmart.com>
Refdesk <http://www.refdesk.com>
The WWW Virtual Library <http://vlib.org>
Yahoo! <http://www.yahoo.com>

shown in Figure 1.2, you can select a subject collection to browse, or search for keywords in all the collections. By searching for information on biological warfare, for example, you would discover that INFOMINE recommends about thirty-six sites for your inspection. (See Figure 4.7 on page 107.) The links on the research results screen take you to individual sites, lead you to related resources, and invite you to post your own comments.

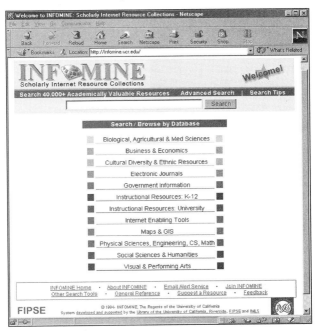

Figure 1.2
The homepage of INFOMINE
<http://infomine.ucr.edu>

If you click the homepage link "About INFOMINE," you will find the following description: "INFOMINE is a virtual library of Internet resources relevant to faculty, students, and research staff at the university level. It contains useful Internet resources like databases, electronic journals, electronic books, bulletin boards, mailing lists, online library card catalogs, articles, directories of researchers, and many other types of information. INFOMINE is librarian built." See 4c-7 for further information about INFOMINE's features.

The Internet Public Library
<http://www.ipl.org>

The homepage of the Internet Public Library (IPL) recalls the lobby of a real library, with links to areas such as Reference, Teen, and Youth. According to the IPL's "Mission Statement," "The Internet is a mess. Since nobody runs it, that's no surprise." The librarians propose to clean up the "mess," using their organizing skills to help people find and use information that is interesting and worthwhile. A special feature is the IPL Reference Center at <http://www.ipl.org /ref>. At this site, librarians will answer your questions by email.

Librarian's Index to the Internet
<http://lii.org>

Begun in 1990 as a personal set of Gopher bookmarks, the Librarian's Index has evolved into a collection of links to 10,000 Web pages on all topics, monitored by more than 100 California librarians. Each link features an annotation written by one of these librarians, describing the resource and explaining its value.

Refdesk
<http://www.refdesk.com>

Refdesk is a one-stop center for everything a Web researcher might need. On the homepage you'll find links to worldwide news sources, reference tools such as dictionaries and calendars, and Web editions of hundreds of international magazines and newspapers. The "Ask the Experts" link leads to a list of more than 140 sites where you can post questions to experts who will answer you either by email or on their site.

Yahoo!
<http://www.yahoo.com>

Yahoo! is one of the most popular subject-directory search tools. Its **homepage**, shown in Figure 1.3, offers links to more than a dozen major categories such as Arts and Humanities, Education, Entertainment, Health, Recreation and Sports, Reference, and Society and Culture. After opening a category, you keep choosing from successive menus until you reach a list of Web sites you may want to visit. Or, using the dialog box on the Yahoo! main screen, you can retrieve Yahoo! categories containing specific keywords, or individual sites whose titles or short descriptions contain your keywords. The list of **hits** for a Yahoo! search also offers links to other search tools.

For example, if you wanted information about Mount Everest, you could easily focus your search by clicking on the Environment and Nature link and following it to Mountains and then Mount Everest. That last link would produce a list of Everest-related Web sites much like the one in Figure 1.4. A subject directory such as Yahoo! makes an excellent starting point when you know your destination.

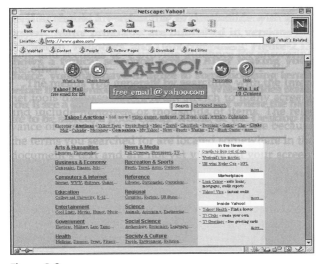

Figure 1.3
The homepage for Yahoo!
<http://www.yahoo.com>

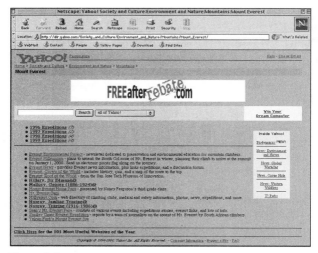

Figure 1.4
A search results screen from Yahoo!

Other subject-directory search tools   At LookSmart, The
WWW Virtual Library, and the Library of Congress
homepage, you'll find guides to Web resources for
hundreds of subject areas. LookSmart at <http://www
.looksmart.com> lists sites by topic, lets you search by
keyword, and offers worldwide directories. The WWW
Virtual Library has links to webliographies arranged
according to the topics used by the Library of Congress.
You'll find the Virtual Library at <http://vlib.org>. To
examine one of the most extensive lists of Internet subject directories, visit the Library of Congress homepage
at <http://lcweb.loc .gov>, which has exceptionally useful links to search tools that provide information on all
Internet sources.

2   Text indexes

If you already know which aspect of a topic you want to
investigate, you can use a search tool that looks through
its **text index** of Internet documents for the **keywords**
you specify and prepares a results menu with links to
documents containing the keywords. These tools create
their indexes by scanning millions of documents and

Box 1.3
Some popular text-indexing search tools

AltaVista <http://www.altavista.com>
Excite <http://excite.com>
Google <http://www.google.com>
HotBot <http://www.hotbot.com>
Lycos <http://www.lycos.com>
Net Search <http://search.netscape.com>
Northern Light Search <http://northernlight.com>
WebCrawler <http://www.webcrawler.com>

recording the occurrence of every word and phrase. Each tool follows unique rules for selecting documents to index, and so the results you get from querying one text index will usually be quite different from the results you'd get with another.

This section describes two of the most useful text-indexing search tools, and Box 1.3 lists a number of others.

AltaVista
<http://www.altavista.com>

One of the most comprehensive Internet search tools, AltaVista indexes the full text of more than 550 million Web pages and several million newsgroup messages. You can perform a "Simple" search using the dialog box on the opening screen, or select an "Advanced" search screen that lets you specify more precise relationships among keywords and request that hits containing certain terms be listed first. You can also specify how much detail the list of hits should include. AltaVista generally gives more extensive results than other search tools, but you may have to look through many menus to find the most relevant items.

Figure 1.5 shows the first few hits resulting from an AltaVista search for the name *Mount Everest* in September 1999. The words, when typed in the dialog box, were enclosed in quotation marks so the search engine would treat them as a phrase. (Had we not used quotation marks, the results would have included all sites containing both words, regardless of their order or proximity. You can

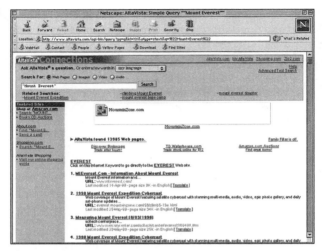

Figure 1.5
Some results of an AltaVista search
<http://www.altavista.com>

use this quotation-mark strategy whenever a search for a multiple-word term returns too many hits.) AltaVista lists the results in sets of ten links per page, with onscreen buttons to click from one set to another.

More complex search strategies can be used with AltaVista's Advanced Search screen, easily reached from the homepage. The Advanced Search dialog box lets you specify relationships between your keywords using certain words and symbols. For example, to find documents where the words *undersea exploration* occur close to *Pacific Ocean,* you might search for the expression *"undersea exploration" NEAR Pacific.* For more on refining your search in this way, see AltaVista's Help screens as well as section 1h and Box 1.5 (on page 36) in *Online!*

Google
<http://www.google.com>

Google indexes more than 1.3 billion Web documents. The main search page has a simple dialog box much like AltaVista's, while the advanced search page lets you specify combinations of search words. Hits are ranked by the frequency and proximity of your search words and by the frequency of links between the documents found. As a result, the top hits are usually very worthwhile. If you enter a street address, Google assumes you want to see a map for that location, and gives map sites the highest priority. In a Google search, you use **quotation marks** to enclose phrases, as with AltaVista, but you cannot perform searches with the **NEAR** qualifier or the **asterisk** (see 1h).

3 Metaengines

A growing number of **metaengines** let you search several Web indexes simultaneously. The metaengine submits your keywords to the other search engines, collects the results, and provides you with a summary of the hits. Two of the easiest-to-use metaengines are Metacrawler at <http://www.metacrawler.com> and Ask Jeeves! at <http://ask.com>. When you enter your keywords into Metacrawler's search box and click the Search button, you get combined results from nine different search tools, including the subject directory Yahoo! and the text indexes AltaVista and Excite. Metacrawler automatically sorts the hits to remove duplicates and ranks them by relevance. When you Ask Jeeves! a question, the search tool looks for closely related searches among the questions it has answered before and offers you those results along with menus of the hits from other text indexes.

Because each metaengine limits the number of hits it gathers from individual tools, typically accepting only the first ten, you can't depend on the results of a metasearch to be comprehensive. However, metasearches often give excellent results when you are searching for very general topics or for information about very current events. Box 1.4 lists the URLs for some popular metaengines.

Box 1.4
Some popular metaengines

AllTheWeb <http://www.alltheweb.com>
AltaVista <http://www.altavista.com>
Ask Jeeves! <http://www.ask.com>
Dogpile <http://www.dogpile.com>
Metacrawler <http://www.metacrawler.com>
Search.com <http://www.search.com>
Teoma <http://www.teoma.com>

4 Subject-specific search engines

When you need to restrict your Internet searching to documents within a limited subject field, consider using a search engine devoted to that subject. You can find an extensive list of subject-specific tools at Easy Searcher <http://www.easysearcher.com>. Figure 1.6 shows Easy Searcher's homepage when the link for tools in Arts/Humanities/Languages has been clicked.

For more examples of subject-specific tools, consult Appendix B.

1h Refining your search

To refine or limit your search, go to your **search tool**'s Help command (accessible directly from most search tools' screens). AltaVista's Help link, for example, suggests many ways to broaden or restrict searches. Suppose you want to explore Web sites offering information on undersea exploration. A text search for such

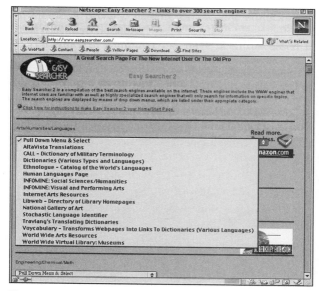

Figure 1.6
Easy Searcher's subject indexes for Arts, Humanities, and Languages
<http://www.easysearcher.com>

sites in June 2002 turned up more than 107,000 documents containing the word *undersea* and more than 2.4 million documents containing the word *exploration*. When the search was narrowed to *undersea exploration*, the query produced just 1,459 documents containing the phrase. When the search was further narrowed to look for the words *Pacific Ocean* within those 1,459 documents, the field shrank to 37 documents—a very manageable number of sources to examine closely! While each search tool has its own means for refining or restricting a search, you should always be able to find a Help or Tips screen that explains the options.

Search tools often allow you to refine your search by doing one or more of the following:

- Requiring or excluding keywords
- Limiting where the keywords are sought within pages (e.g., in the title, the text, or the URL)
- Limiting searching to Web, newsgroup, or FTP items
- Requiring or excluding documents from particular Internet sites or domains

If your search results are either too numerous for convenient reviewing or too few for your needs, see whether a closely related term produces more useful results. Using a wild-card technique (e.g., searching for *immigra** rather than *immigration*) usually generates more hits, while narrowing your topic by adding more search terms usually draws the most relevant hits to the top of the stack. Excite, AltaVista, and many other tools let you use specific words and symbols (see Box 1.5) to determine how terms should be related. You can also try a different search tool. (See 1g-2 for more on these tools.) Different search tools will give you different results, since each tool has its own strategy and its own database.

To narrow a search with a text index, you can use words and symbols known as **logical operators**. For example, when you want to look for a phrase consisting of two or more keywords, enclose them in quotation marks, as in *"undersea exploration."* The words **AND**, **OR**, and **NOT**—commonly called **Boolean operators**—let you specify which terms must, may, or must not occur in the documents you want to retrieve. For example, searching for *Rainier AND summit* will retrieve all documents containing both of those words, whether the documents pertain to Mount Rainier or to the prince of Monaco; searching for *Rainier AND summit NOT prince* will return many of the same hits, but the list will now exclude those that mention *prince*. A search for *Rainier OR summit* retrieves all documents that contain at least one—or both—of the keywords. Many search tools also let you use the operator **NEAR** and the symbols **"" (quotation marks)**, **+ (the plus sign)**, **– (the minus sign)**, and *** (the asterisk)** to narrow your search. For a summary of frequently used logical operators, see Box 1.5.

Not all text indexes permit the use of all these words and symbols. For more information, check the Help or Advanced Search option of the search engine you are using.

Box 1.5
Refining text index searches

Use the following words and symbols for more effective searches with text indexes.

AND Locates documents containing both keywords, in any order: *undersea AND exploration*

OR Locates documents containing one or both keywords: *undersea OR exploration*

NOT Excludes documents that contain the keyword: *NOT undersea*

NEAR (not available in all search engines) Locates documents where the keywords occur close together: *undersea NEAR exploration*

" " Locates documents containing the phrase that is in quotation marks: *"undersea exploration"*

+ Locates only documents that contain the specified keyword or phrase: *+undersea* or *+"undersea exploration"*

- Similar to NOT; excludes documents containing the keyword or phrase: *-exploration* or *-"undersea exploration"*

* When placed after a word or part of a word, locates documents containing words that start with that combination of letters: *explor** will locate documents containing *exploration, explorer, exploratory,* and so on

Connecting to the Internet

When your personal computer is connected to the **Internet**, you use a **graphic browser** such as Netscape Communicator or Microsoft Internet Explorer to view Web pages and participate in Web discussion forums. (Figures 2.1 and 2.2 show the basic onscreen features of these two browsers.) You use an **email** program—either one integrated with your browser or one that you install separately—to correspond electronically with other Internet users and with **listservs**. You can also use your browser or specialized software to participate in **newsgroups** and **real-time communication** (e.g., in **chats**, **MOOs** and electronic conferences). This chapter gives guidelines for accessing these and other types of Internet sources.

Security indicator   Status line   Mail button   Screen scroll bar

Navigation buttons   Links to select   Location bar

Figure 2.1
A screen in Netscape Communicator
<http://netscape.com>

2a   Getting connected

When choosing your Internet connection, you have
several options. Most home and small-business users
connect their personal computers by **modems** to their
Internet service provider (ISP) through ordinary telephone lines, digital subscriber lines (DSL), and cable
television connections. Many businesses and schools
have **local area networks (LANs)** that permit speedier
Internet connections. Wireless networks providing fast
connections for home use are also becoming widely
available.

2b   Using the World Wide Web

The **World Wide Web**—often called the Web—is a network of **hypertext** documents. (See 1c for a fuller description of the Web.) Each document has an "address" called
a **URL (uniform resource locator)**. (See 1d.) Web page
URLs always begin with the **HTTP protocol**, which
appears in URLs as *http://*. For accessing URLs, most

Links to select

Navigation buttons

Screen scroll bar

Location bar

Mail

Figure 2.2
A screen in Microsoft Internet Explorer
<http://www.msn.com>

graphic browsers provide a **dialog box** or **location bar**—
which might be labeled "Location" or "Go To" or "Net-
site"—with space for typing in a full HTTP address. To
reach a Web site whose URL you know, type the URL
into the box and press Enter. (If you're working from
within another text that contains the URL you want to
reach, use your computer's Copy and Paste commands
to insert the URL into the box.)

For example, to reach the **Web site** of Project Gutenberg, which is making classic texts available in electronic format, you would type:

▶ http://www.promo.net/pg

Figure 2.3 shows the Project Gutenberg **homepage**. With
many browsers you don't have to type *http://* at the
beginning of a URL; the browser automatically inserts
the prefix for you.

A key feature of browser navigation is the use of
bookmarks or **favorites** to record the URLs of sites you
may want to visit again. To compile a **bookmark list**
while visiting a site, use a menu option or screen button

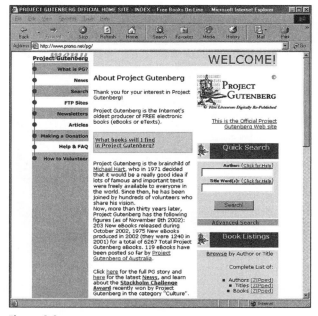

Figure 2.3
The Project Gutenberg homepage
<http://www.promo.net/pg>

to save a bookmark, which stores the address and lets you return quickly to the site later by selecting its entry from your bookmark list. If you share a computer with other users, you can save your bookmarks to a file, store the file on a floppy disk, and later import it to the browser again.

When you subscribe with an **Internet service provider**, you usually receive an installation software package that includes one or both of the popular browsers. If you use America Online, Earthlink, or Juno, the opening screen will offer Web links, advertisements, and other services to their subscribers. These offers, while occasionally useful, do not always include the most up-to-date Web technologies. For best performance with Web pages, start a true browser program after your computer makes a connection with such an ISP.

To work most effectively, your browser may require additional pieces of software commonly called **plug-ins**; it will alert you to the need for such software and even lead you through the process of downloading and installing it.

Here are the homepages of the popular browsers:

Microsoft Internet Explorer
<http://www.microsoft.com>

Netscape Communicator and Netscape Navigator
<http://www.netscape.com>

You can browse the Web—moving from one document to another—in any of four ways:

- Clicking links on the currently open page
- Typing the URL for another page into the dialog box or location bar
- Selecting a bookmark, toolbar button, or menu item
- Searching for pages that meet your criteria

All of these methods are available to you as soon as you start your browser.

Most browsing software is preset to take you to its **portal** (gateway site) when you launch the program. You can usually customize a portal to present your preferred news sites, sports scores, stock quotations, weather reports, and the like. Box 2.1 lists the URLs of several popular portals.

If you'd rather start with the homepage of your school or community, or your favorite search tool, select that page by following these directions: For Netscape Communicator, open the Edit menu, select Preferences, highlight Navigator, and type the URL you have in mind on the "Home page" line. For Microsoft Internet Explorer, open the View menu, select Internet Options, click the General tab, and type the URL on the Address line.

Box 2.1
Some popular portals to the World Wide Web

Excite <http://www.excite.com>

GO Network <http://www.go.com>

Lycos <http://www.lycos.com>

MSN <http://www.msn.com>

NBCi <http://www.nbci.com>

Netscape Netcenter <http://www.netscape.com>

Yahoo! <http://www.yahoo.com>

Use your browser's buttons, menus, and toolbars to navigate the Web. If the function of a button isn't obvious, hold the cursor over it and wait a second or two for a helpful word or phrase to pop up. Consult the Help menu for additional suggestions. For help with using URLs and search tools while you browse, see 1d–h. For help with **downloading** material from the Web to your computer, see 2j.

2c Using email

Email (electronic mail) works like the postal system (only much faster!), transmitting messages to individuals and groups over computer networks. While you'll find many personal uses for email, in your research you will most likely use it for the following:

- Requesting information about authors and sources
- Exchanging word-processed documents and other files
- Using email links in **Web** documents
- Using **listservs**

Graphic browsers include all normal mail-handling functions. For example, with Netscape Communicator you can select the Netscape Messenger window, then read or send messages. Microsoft Internet Explorer includes the free email program Outlook Express. If you buy and install Microsoft Office, you will automatically install Microsoft Outlook in place of Outlook Express. Microsoft Outlook includes several information management features not present in Outlook Express, but the email functions of the two programs are very similar.

1 Sending and reading messages

Sending an email message usually involves little more than clicking on a New Message button or menu item; typing the recipient's address, a **subject line**, and your text; and clicking a Send button. Your name and email address are automatically included in the message **header**. To read an incoming message, you click an entry in a list and see the message in its own window. Figures 2.4, 2.5, and 2.6 show typical email sending and reading screens.

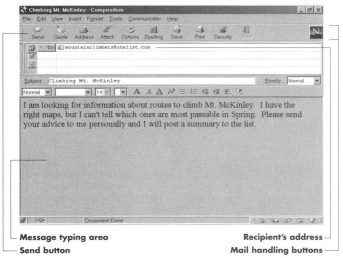

Message typing area

Send button

Recipient's address

Mail handling buttons

Figure 2.4
Sending email in Netscape Messenger

Most email programs enable you to use the following special functions:

CC:—A line in the header that lets you send a "carbon copy" of your message to a third party

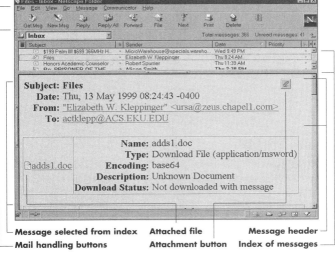

Message selected from index

Mail handling buttons

Attached file

Attachment button

Message header

Index of messages

Figure 2.5
Reading email with an attachment in Netscape Messenger

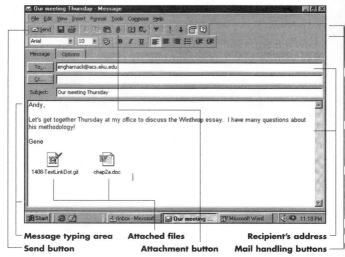

Message typing area   **Attached files**   **Recipient's address**
Send button   **Attachment button**   **Mail handling buttons**

Figure 2.6
Sending email with attachments in Microsoft Outlook

Attachments—Files such as word-processed documents, graphics, or spreadsheets that you want to include with your message

Hypertext links—URLs you type into your message that appear on your recipient's screen as active links, ready to be followed

Signature file—Lines of text (and/or a graphic) that are automatically added to the end of every message you send (for example, you might include your name, your title, your school's or company's name, your address, and any other contact information)

Address book—A way of storing your collection of email addresses

2 Working with attachments

Most browser email programs let you send **attachments** with your email messages. For example, in Netscape Messenger and Microsoft Outlook, when you send a file along with an email message, you begin (as usual) by addressing the message, typing a subject, and writing your message's text. To attach the file, click the Attach button, which may be labeled with a paper-clip icon (see Figures 2.6 and 2.7). Then select the file you want to send and click OK. Repeat this process if you have more than

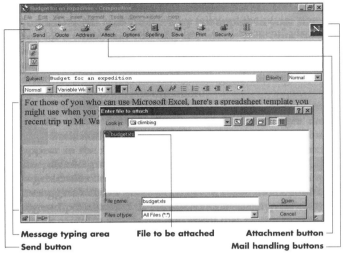

Message typing area   File to be attached   Attachment button
Send button   Mail handling buttons

Figure 2.7
Composing email with an attachment in Netscape Messenger

one file to send. In the message itself, be sure to tell your recipient what you are attaching, and then send the message as usual. After opening your message, your recipient will be able to view or save the contents of the file.

Your email recipients need to know what kind of files they are receiving so they can use the right software to view and save them. Pictures and other graphics in **GIF** or **JPEG** formats (i.e., with the **extensions** *.gif* or *.jpg*) pose no problems, since all graphic browsers can display them. By contrast, word-processed files, spreadsheets, and databases can generally be opened only with the program in which they were created, although some programs do recognize and convert files from other formats. If you and your recipients have different versions of the same program (e.g., Microsoft Word 97 and Word 2000), you can still exchange files easily if the user of the more recent program saves documents in the older program's format (a feature of the Save As menu selection) before attaching them. As you create files to exchange with others, be sure to use *standard fonts* (fonts included with your computer's operating system) so that your documents appear to your recipients as you intend them to. If you plan to send a long or complicated document, first email a shorter document and verify that your recipient can read it.

Your email program uses several visual cues to alert you when a message has an attachment. You may see a paper-clip icon near the message's entry in your Inbox list, or a similar indicator in the message-reading window (as in Figure 2.5, on page 43), or a file icon or link at the end of the message (as in Figure 2.6). If a picture or other graphic appears within the message, you can work with it by **right-clicking** over it. Netscape Communicator users can **toggle** the Attachment Pane (see Figure 2.5), which displays the icons for all files attached to a message.

If you click on the icon or link for an attachment, your browser will ask whether you want to save the file or open it. Choosing to save the file is generally wise because it allows you to use the file more conveniently outside your email, and it helps avoid contaminating your system with viruses (see 2c-3). Be sure to save files to a location where you can find them easily, such as the desktop or the My Documents folder. Figure 2.8 shows how a screen may look when an attachment is being saved to the desktop.

After saving an attachment, you can use it as you would any other file. Take care to observe the virus protection procedures described in 2c-3.

For more on using email, see 3c-2.

3 Eluding computer viruses

Viruses cannot infect your computer while you are browsing the Web or reading or sending email. Of

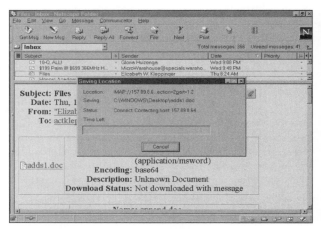

Figure 2.8
Saving an email attachment to the desktop

course, you may unknowingly already have a virus and be spreading it to your email recipients. Your computer becomes infected either by running an already infected program you received from someone else or by using its installed software—such as your word-processor—to open an already infected file. For example, if someone sends you a Microsoft Word file containing a *macro virus* (a virus that affects macros), you will not infect your system by reading the message or saving the attachment, but you will get the virus if you open the file itself with Microsoft Word—unless you have taken proper precautions.

Some viruses may seem to cause only minor annoyance, such as changing the name of your hard drive (as seen in the My Computer window). (An infamous example is the GROOV macro virus, which is easily diagnosed when your hard drive's name suddenly changes to "Groovie.") The real danger of a virus is the invisible damage it can do, such as infecting the file template that your word processor uses whenever you create and save files. From that point on, until you disinfect (that is, remove the virus from) your system, every document you open, new or old, will be infected and thus be capable of infecting other computers. Most of the destructive capabilities of viruses have been aimed at Windows computers, but Macintosh viruses also exist. Macro viruses infect files readily in either environment, even though their destructive effects may be limited to one system. For example, a Macintosh user may open an infected Microsoft Word file and notice nothing wrong, but Word files from this system now represent potential threats to correspondents using Windows. Viruses have even been designed to replicate by automatically emailing themselves (as attachments, of course) to addresses listed in a user's electronic **address book**.

In addition to self-propagation, many viruses attack their host system, changing or corrupting its programs and files, often beyond repair. To protect yourself against viruses, follow these steps:

- Install antivirus software that automatically updates itself as new viruses are discovered. Programs such as Norton AntiVirus and McAfee Virus Scan are readily available through computer stores and online retailers.

- Set up your antivirus software to scan your files automatically so that it can detect any suspicious files as they are received.

- Make sure that the virus protection features built into software programs such as Microsoft's Word, Excel, PowerPoint, and Access are enabled (turned on). If you try to open a potentially infected file while protection is in effect, you'll see a pop-up box warning you that the file may be infected. The warning box lets you choose to (1) open the file with macros disabled (a safe action), (2) open the file with macros enabled (an action that may be unsafe), or (3) cancel the operation. Note that under these conditions you will see a warning every time you get a file that contains macros. Many macros have legitimate uses; if you know your macros are safe, simply open the file. For maximum virus protection inside an application such as Microsoft Word, you must make your templates uninfectable by setting the Read-Only file property.

- When working with an email attachment, *never* choose to open the attachment directly; otherwise, you may override the virus protection features you have installed.

- Learn more about viruses and their disinfection at the Web sites listed at the end of this section.

If someone sends you an email alert about a supposed virus, don't automatically forward the alert to others. Most virus alerts are hoaxes, and their main effect is to create more and more email as the forwarding proliferates. If you are concerned about the alert, forward it to your organization's help desk or to your **ISP**, so that its validity can be evaluated. For more on virus alerts, see the F-Secure Anti-Virus Hoax Warnings Page at <http://www.f-secure.com/news/hoax>.

For more information about viruses, visit one of these sites:

CERT Coordination Center
<http://www.cert.org>

F-Secure Security Information Center
<http://www.f-secure.com/virus-info>

McAfee.com: Virus Information Library
<http://vil.mcafee.com>

Symantec Security Response
<http://www.symantec.com/avcenter>

2d Using Web discussion forums

Web discussion forums are sites designed to facilitate online debate and information exchange. Their structure incorporates features of several other kinds of Internet sources:

- Like most Web pages, these sites have **hypertext** links and graphics.
- Like **email** (see 2c), the messages you can read have a personal tone, usually including names and email addresses.
- As in **newsgroups** (see 2f), the discussion follows threads that are displayed onscreen as a series of messages and replies.

In the discussion forum shown in Figure 2.9, each **article** has an ordinary-looking *http:* URL that lets you retrieve the article as you would any other Web page (i.e., by clicking on an onscreen link or typing into a dialog box). To see how an article might look, examine Figure 2.10. On the article's display screen, buttons make it easy to link back to the list of articles, comment on the article, or read comments by others. The article list in Figure 2.9 shows how the discussion forum format preserves

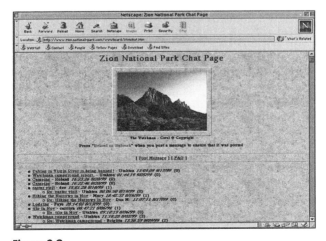

Figure 2.9
Part of the hierarchy of messages from the Zion National Park Chat Page
<http://www.zion.national-park.com/wwwboard/zionchat.htm>

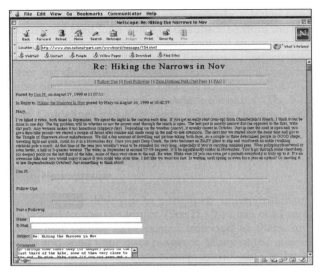

Figure 2.10
One of the discussion messages listed in Figure 2.9

threads (series of articles about a particular topic) and lets you contribute responses that immediately appear as new articles under the relevant thread heading. In short, a discussion forum page gives you access both to an ongoing conversation and to the conversation's history.

Your **graphic browser** provides all the functions you need to access discussion forums.

2e Using listservs

Listservs are ongoing **email** discussions about technical or nontechnical issues, covering the spectrum from aboriginal languages to zoology. Messages are typically announcements, questions, position statements, or replies and are distributed to the personal email boxes of all of the listserv's subscribers.

In order to start receiving a particular listserv's **postings**, you must subscribe to the listserv from your own email account. *Important: Never send a listserv subscription request to the list's own address.* Listservs have a separate address for handling subscriptions, and subscribers understandably become annoyed when they must sort out subscription requests from useful messages. As you uncover interesting listservs, pay careful attention to the *separate addresses for subscribing to a list and for sending messages to the list.*

For example, to subscribe to the Macintosh News and Information list, you would send the message *subscribe MAC-L* [your name] to <listproc@lehigh.edu>. To send messages to the list members, you would use the address <mac-l@lehigh.edu>. With some listservs, you subscribe via a Web site instead of email. For example, to subscribe to the BackpackingLight list, you would visit Yahoo! Groups at <http://groups.yahoo.com> and follow the directions. To send messages to list members, you'd use the address <BackpackingLight@yahoogroups .com>. You can find more information about listservs through the "Internet Mailing Lists: Guides and Resources" page at <http://www.ifla.org/I/training /listservs/lists.htm>, as well as excellent listserv indexes at Tile.Net <http://www.tile.net> and the "Directory of Publicity Accessible Mailing Lists" at <http://paml .net>.

Listservs include *open lists* (to which anyone may subscribe and **post** messages), *moderated lists* (where a human **moderator** reviews messages before they go to subscribers), and *closed lists* (where you must request permission or explain your goals before being permitted to join). Discussions may range from technical analyses of narrow topics to friendly brainstorming. After subscribing to a listserv, observe the message traffic for a few days (or review the list's **archives**) to get a feel for the list's "personality" before contributing your own message. With most unmoderated lists, *anything* you send to the list address is forwarded immediately to every subscriber.

See 3c-3 for more on using listservs.

2f Using newsgroups

The **Usenet** network provides access to many thousands of electronic discusssion groups called **newsgroups**. Unlike **listserv** messages (see 2e), which are delivered to your private **email** box, Usenet messages are collected on a system called a *news server,* where anyone with access to Usenet can retrieve them.

Here is a typical newsgroup name:

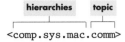

The first part of the name specifies the Usenet *hierarchy* (category) to which the group belongs—in this case, *comp.* for computer-related topics. A **dot** separates the hierarchy from the rest of the name, which specifies the newsgroup's topic through successively narrower sub-hierarchies—in this case, communications programs for Macintosh computer systems.

There are hundreds of Usenet hierarchies. Major ones besides *comp.* include *news.* for Usenet information, *rec.* for recreational activities and hobbies, *sci.* for scientific topics, *soc.* for social, political, and religious subjects, *talk.* for opinion, and *misc.* and *alt.* for topics that don't fit elsewhere.

Graphic browsers will accept URLs containing the *news:* **protocol**, as in <news:alt.adoption>, provided your browser's Options or Preferences screens specify a news server. (If you need to specify your news server, try the address of your mail server or ask your system staff or **Internet service provider** for help.) Some browsers provide a separate window with Usenet-oriented functions. The browser retrieves and displays the messages you seek; it may also let you post your own messages.

If you can't use your browser to access news-groups, you may be able to use a *newsreader* program; try News Xpress at <http://cws.internet.com/news-nxpress.html> or NewsWatcher for Macintosh at <ftp://ftp.tidbits.com/pub/tidbits/select/newswatcher.hqx>, or ask a computer expert for help.

For advice on participating in newsgroups, see 3c-4.

2g Using real-time communication

In the simplest form of **real-time communication**, two people chat online by typing "instant" messages to each other's computer screens, using software that displays each message sequentially. Two popular instant-messag-

ing programs are ICQ ("I seek you"), downloadable at
<http://web.icq.com>, and AIM (AOL Instant Messenger), downloadable at <http://www.aim.com>. These
programs let you save transcripts of your conversations
much as you would record a telephone call. You can also
exchange files with your chat partners and leave messages for them to retrieve when they connect.

Chat programs also provide online "rooms" at their
Web sites where groups of people can converse. ICQ and
AIM offer permanent chat rooms and also let you create
your own rooms as needed. Similar features are available through Excite Chat at <http://communicate.excite
.com/chat/html> and Yahoo! Chat at <http://chat/yahoo
.com>. Conversations in chat rooms resemble instant-messaging sessions, but chat rooms are usually organized as public sites where anyone may enter to lurk or
participate.

Among the most potent expressions of Internet interactivity are **MUDs** and **MOOs**, which provide electronic
"spaces" where people can "meet." **MUD** stands for
multi-user domain. If a MUD is *object-oriented* (meaning
that you can type commands to create and manipulate
virtual objects—tables, pets, or anything imaginable), it's
called a **MOO (multi-user domain, object-oriented)**.

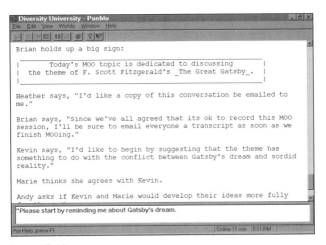

Figure 2.11
A fragment of conversation at Diversity University MOO
<telnet://moo.duets.org:8888>

These forms of virtual reality on the Internet are frequently used for online classes and conferences. Right now almost all MUD and MOO communication is limited to text (see Figure 2.11), although some sites are adding a graphic window to integrate pictures or video with the typed conversation.

The **URL** for a MUD or MOO site begins with the *telnet://*protocol and usually ends with a port number. Here's the URL for Diversity University MOO:

Your browser can open such a URL as long as it can find a **telnet** program (see 2h-3), but there are drawbacks to telnetting to a MUD or MOO through your browser: your screen shows all messages as a continuous flow, and your own typing sometimes gets interrupted by others' messages, with very confusing results. If you must use this method, get advice from Nick Carbone's document "Telnet Help Sheet for MOOing" at <http://www.daedalus.com/net/telnet.html>.

Some MOOs can be accessed via the Web, with its graphic capabilities. For example, if you visit Diversity University MOO through its Web- and telnet-integrated **interface** at <http://moo.duets.org:8888>, you will see a screen like Figure 2.12, where the top section uses graphics and the lower section displays the ongoing conversation as text. For a list of educational MOOs, many of which now offer Web interfaces, see "Rachel's Super MOO List: Educational MOOs" at <http://moolist.yeehaw.net/edu.html>.

For frequent MUD or MOO exploration, you may want to use a **client** program that gives you better control over what you type and what you see onscreen. Many client programs are available for Macintosh, Unix, and Windows systems; for reviews, see Jennifer Smith's "Frequently Asked/Answered Questions" at <http://www.mudconnect.com/mudfaq>. The *Online!* Web site offers links to download several MUD/MOO clients. Web pages that give information about basic MUD/MOO commands and describe various sites include "Don't Be Cowed by the MOO" at <http://www.csun.edu/~hceng028/MOO.html>, Traci Gardner's "MOO Teacher's Tip Sheet" at <http://www.daedalus

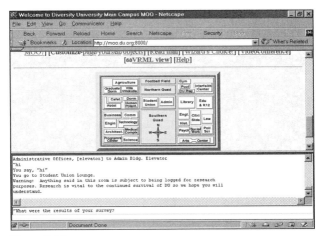

Figure 2.12
**Diversity University MOO's Web- and telnet-integrated
interface**
<http://moo.du.org:8000>

.com/net/MOOTIPS.html>, and Lydia Leong's "The
MUD Resource Collection" at <http://www.godlike.com
/muds>.

Section 3c-5 gives advice on participating in real-time
communication.

2h Using FTP, gopher, and telnet

FTP (file transfer protocol), **gopher**, and **telnet** are
older Internet **protocols** whose importance has been
diminished—at least from the user's perspective—by
Web **interfaces** and **browser** improvements. This section provides detailed directions for dealing with problems you may encounter when using sources whose
URL begins with *ftp://*, *gopher://*, or *telnet://*.

1 FTP

FTP (file transfer protocol) transports files between
computers on the Internet. Here's a typical FTP site URL:

You can type the URL command into your browser's dialog box. If you have only a site name, such as <ftp .tidbits.com>, construct a usable URL with the *ftp://* prefix: <ftp://ftp.tidbits.com>. If your browser responds "invalid URL" when you specify a site name, try adding a forward slash at the end of the URL: thus, <ftp:// wuarchive.wustl.edu> becomes <ftp://wuarchive.wustl .edu/>.

The most common use for FTP is **downloading** software such as updates or **plug-ins** for your existing programs and for new programs you want to try. Computer hardware manufacturers often place improved software for their devices on their Web sites for FTP delivery to their customers.

If you get a "login incorrect" message after attempting an FTP connection through your browser, the other computer did not accept your browser's automatic method for anonymous identification. (Most FTP servers expect your computer to use *anonymous* as your username and your email address as your password.) Consider using a separate FTP program (see the end of this section for advice), or try typing the expected identification as a URL in your browser's dialog box, according to the following special pattern:

▶ ftp://anonymous:username%40system.dom@ftphost
name.dom

The symbols %40 in the pattern represent the @ sign in your email address. (The @ sign itself has a different meaning when it appears in a URL.)

Although browsers are designed to handle FTP, you may have trouble in particular situations. One frequent problem with FTP arises when files in *binary* format are mistakenly transferred as *text* files, or vice versa. Binary files, such as programs or program archives, images, and formatted files from word processors and spreadsheets, transfer more slowly than text files. Efficient file transfer depends on knowing the proper format for each file. The FTP process itself can't determine which kind of data a particular file contains; instead, it predicts which format to use from the **extension** (final element) in the file's name, such as *.zip, .txt,* or *.html.* Currently, **graphic browsers** don't let you override these predictions, and so the transfer of a file with an inappropriate or unusual extension may fail or may make the file useless to you. If you have trouble using FTP through your usual browser, consider getting a separate program such as Fetch (for Macintosh) or WS_FTP Pro (for Windows) for FTP. You can find Fetch at <ftp://ftp.tidbits.com/pub/tidbits/select/fetch.hqx> and WS_FTP Pro at <http://www.ipswitch.com/products /WS_FTP>.

For more information about using FTP, including detailed instructions for saving various kinds of files, see the document "How to Use FTP" at <http://www .brandx.net/help/ftp-howto.html>.

2 Gopher

Gopher, a program for accessing Internet information through menus arranged in hierarchies, will "go for" the information you seek and will display it on your screen. Gopher **URLs** look very much like **HTTP** and **FTP** addresses but usually contain a crucial one- or two-digit number that specifies the *type* of resource being selected, rather than just naming a file **directory**. For example, in the imaginary URL

▶ `<gopher: //domain.name.edu/7data/findit>`

the 7 signals a request to use the *findit* search within the *data* directory. Gopher selection pathways often involve characters, especially spaces, that are not allowed in standard URLs and so must be translated with special symbols, resulting in unwieldy strings like <gopher:// gopher.tc.umn.edu/00/Information%20About%20 Gopher/about>.

For URLs that begin with the *gopher:* protocol, use your regular Web browser. With a very complicated URL, you may find it useful to reach the "root" gopher by typing only the protocol and full server name (in this case, <gopher://gopher.tc.umn.edu>). When you reach the gopher site, use the menus to find the document by deciphering the correct screen selections from the remainder of the URL.

If you're not satisfied with your Web browser's handling of gopher sources, consider using a separate program such as WSGopher for Windows at <ftp://boom box.micro.umn.edu/pub/gopher/Windows/wsg-12.exe> or TurboGopher for Macintosh at <ftp://boombox.micro .umn.edu/pub/gopher/Macintosh-TurboGopher>.

3 Telnet

Telnet is an Internet **protocol** that lets you log onto another computer from your computer. When you type a **URL** such as

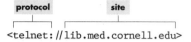

into your **browser**'s window, the browser connects to the site using a separate telnet program on your system. If you don't already have a telnet program, you can get one directly from the Internet via **FTP** (at no cost) through the *Online!* Web site or from <http://download.com.com /3150-2155-0.html?tag=dir>.

Web pages occasionally include telnet links, with onscreen instructions for their use. Knowing how to use telnet is also important when you want to connect through the Internet to run programs on a computer other than the one you're seated at (e.g., to use your campus account while you're away from school).

A telnet session opens in a new window on your screen. This window has no graphics and may show a blinking cursor awaiting your keyboard command. (Telnet can't send instructions from your computer's mouse to the computer you're trying to reach, although you may be able to use your mouse with your own software to highlight text on the screen in order to save it, print it, or copy it for use in your word processor.) Once you're connected, watch for a message about an *escape character*; knowing the character will make it easy to end the connection when you're finished. As the session begins, you may get further instructions (e.g., "login as *visitor* and use password *guest*").

To end a telnet session, type the other computer system's escape command. If no command is listed, try *exit* or *quit* or press ^] or ^C (where ^ means that you hold down the Control key).

2i Using a terminal connection

You have a **terminal connection** (sometimes called *shell* or *indirect access*) if you use a personal computer or networked terminal to log onto another computer (sometimes called a *local host*) and run programs on that computer. You start the connection either from your network or by using communication software such as HyperTerminal, Kermit, ProComm, QModem, or ZTerm to dial your **modem**. The local host then prompts you to enter your **username** and **password**. During your session, you type commands at a prompt (such as a $ sign, a % sign, or a system name) or make selections from an onscreen menu. Your menu choices typically include Mail, Pine, Lynx, **FTP**, **gopher**, and **telnet** (and perhaps **WWW**, for **World Wide Web**). Your account entitles you to use a specific amount of disk space (often called your *quota*) for storing your own files at the other computer. The main limitation of terminal connections is that they don't provide a **graphic interface**, which means that although you can access the text of Web documents, you can't see or use any graphics they may include.

Although terminal accounts don't connect you to the graphics and sound available on the Web, they do have some advantages. First, they're usually free (since they tend to be provided by colleges, universities, and libraries). Furthermore, while **graphic browsers** such as Microsoft Internet Explorer and Netscape Communicator let you see the exciting visual displays that often accompany information, many researchers prefer to use *text-only* browsers such as Lynx, which retrieve information more quickly, bypassing the slowdown of **downloading** graphics. Even some researchers who do have graphic connections turn off their browser's ability to retrieve images so that they can gather Internet information more efficiently and print it (or copy it into other documents) more quickly.

Most software for terminal access is built to use *vt100 terminal emulation,* meaning that the software expects to receive commands typed at a terminal keyboard. Find the vt100 setting on your communication program's menu and use it. If you have trouble connecting, get help from your system staff or consider changing your communication software.

The most popular Web browser for terminal connections is Lynx. To access Lynx, type *lynx* at your system prompt, or select Lynx from your menu. The first time you use Lynx, go to the Options screen (press *o*) to name your **bookmark list** and record your **email address**, and then save your changes (press >).

When working with Lynx, you use keyboard commands, not mouse movements, to control its operations. For example, when you are using **hyperlinks**, which appear as highlighted text on your screen, you press the Down Arrow key to select the next available link and the Right Arrow key to retrieve the information from that link. Box 2.2 gives directions for using Lynx to connect to the *Online!* Web site, which offers more help with using Lynx as your browser. For more information about Lynx, see "Extremely Lynx" at <http://linux4u .jinr.ru/usoft/WWW/www_crl.com/subir/lynx.html>.

Other programs available for terminal use usually include the following:

- An **email** program such as Mail, Pine, or Elm for access to personal email (see 2c) and **listservs** (see 2e)

- A program such as TRN, NN, or News for access to **newsgroups** (see 2f)

- **Telnet**, a program for connecting to other systems for special services such as **real-time communication** (see 2h-3 and 2g)

- **FTP**, the standard program for moving files from one system to another (see 2h-1)

- **Gopher**, a program for accessing Internet information through menus arranged in hierarchies (see 2h-2)

Detailed directions for using these programs are available on the *Online!* Web site, which you can reach through Lynx. (See Box 2.2.)

Box 2.2
Accessing the *Online!* Web site with Lynx

1. Start Lynx.

2. Press *g*; at the bottom of the screen you will see "URL to open:".

3. Type *http://www.bedfordstmartins.com/online* and press Enter; you will see the *Online!* homepage.

4. Press *a* and then *d* to add a bookmark for this site. (If you receive an error message that you have no bookmark file, go to the Options screen by pressing *o*.)

5. Now, whenever you are using Lynx, you can go to the *Online!* site by pressing *v* and selecting the appropriate link.

2j Downloading software

As you work with Internet sources, you will sometimes need to **download** software or other files—for example, to upgrade your **browser** or other programs, or to participate in educational or business activities. Downloading software usually involves the following steps:

- Locating the files you need
- Saving the files onto your computer
- Unpacking or unzipping the files as needed
- Running the installation program

Box 2.3 defines some specialized terms related to downloading.

You can use Web **search tools** (described in 1g and 1h) to look for software, but often you'll find what you need by visiting the Web site for the manufacturer or organization. For example, to find an updated driver for your Hewlett-Packard printer, visit the company's Web site at <http://www.hp.com> and click the link for Drivers. If you don't know the URL for the manufacturer or organization, search for it with a **subject directory** such as Yahoo! <http://www.yahoo.com>.

When you have found the software you seek, you need to choose a version that is compatible with your system. Many programs are published in versions for Macintosh, Windows, and Unix computers; Figure 2.13 shows a typical selection screen. After making your choice, you may have to agree to some licensing terms before the download actually begins. When it does start, you'll see a **dialog box** that lets you select where the files are to be stored; a good choice would be the Desktop or

---

Box 2.3
Some terms related to downloading

- In a *compacted, compressed, packed,* or *zipped* archive, the files your computer can use have been collapsed and/or specially formatted to speed their transfer.

- After you receive the file, your computer has to restore the files to their correct size and format. This process, called *decompressing, expanding, extracting,* or *unzipping,* is handled by freeware programs such as WinZip and Stuffit Expander.

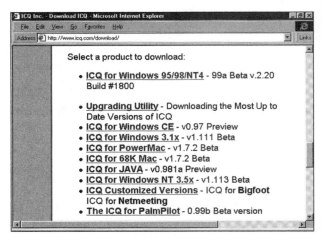

Figure 2.13
Selecting a file to download
<http://www.icq.com/download>

the My Documents folder. As the download progresses, a status bar will keep track of how much information has been transferred.

When the download is complete, look up the file in the location where you stored it, and note its name and **extension**. If the extension is *.exe*, the file is a Windows program and is ready to be used. Similarly, a file with a *.sea* extension is ready for use on a Macintosh. Files with *.zip* extensions are for Windows systems but have been compressed for faster downloading and must be expanded (decompressed) by another program such as WinZip or Stuffit Expander before you can use the contents. Macintosh users need to use Stuffit Expander or a similar program to decompress files with *.bin, .hqx,* or *.sit* extensions. You can download these decompression programs at the following sites:

WinZip (**shareware** for Windows)
<http://www .winzip.com>

Stuffit Expander (**freeware** for Macintosh or Windows)
<http://www.aladdinsys.com>

In the example shown in Figure 2.13, downloading the program for Windows results in a file called <icq.exe>. Double-clicking on the file's icon begins the installation process, after which the ICQ program is ready to run from the Windows Start menu. If the down-loaded file has a *.zip* extension, double-clicking its icon will either start the decompression process or inform you that you need to get a decompression program first.

When a zipped file has been expanded, look for an information file—often called "readme"—to help you use the program, and a Setup or Install file to begin using the software you need.

CHAPTER THREE

Ethics
and
Netiquette

As an **Internet** user, you belong to a **virtual** community along with millions of other **netizens** (Internet citizens). Although the Internet is largely unregulated, the participation of increasing numbers of people has led to a widespread acceptance of certain codes of ethics and conduct. While in most cases no one can force you (or anyone else) to adhere to these codes, if you do so you are more likely to be treated respectfully and helpfully by your fellow netizens, and your work as a writer and researcher will have more credibility. This chapter outlines some of the ethical practices and courtesies practiced by responsible netizens. Because not all Internet users behave responsibly, we also give advice for protecting your privacy and safety online.

3a Observing ethical practices

The Internet enables many people from a variety of cultures to participate in local and global online communities. In order for these communities to flourish, online participants need to show each other the same respect they expect from others offline. Responsible Internet users adopt appropriate *codes of ethics*—principles of conduct by which to live and interact with others.

As a researcher and writer using the Internet to gather new information and ideas, you will encounter a variety of ethical issues. In fact, many schools ask computer users—including students and faculty and staff members—to read and agree to a code of ethics. Such codes emphasize the importance of using computer resources responsibly, honoring the privacy of others, respecting the integrity of institutional databases, and observing high moral standards when accessing other computer systems. (To read the computer-use policies of some educational institutions, see Box 3.1.) In addition, many Internet organizations and commercial sites require that online users agree to codes of conduct that ensure the intellectual, psychological, and emotional safety of others, especially children. For example, participants in Yahoo's communications services, at <http://docs.yahoo.com/info/terms>, promise not to post anything that is "unlawful, harmful, threatening, abusive, harassing, tortious, defamatory, vulgar, obscene, libelous, invasive of another's privacy, hateful, or racially, ethnically or otherwise objectionable."

The ethics of computer use have been discussed in numerous publications. You may find the following sites especially helpful sources of up-to-date information:

Centre for Applied Ethics
<http://www.ethics.ubc.ca/resources/computer>

Box 3.1
Computer-use policies at selected schools

Cornell University
<http://www.cornell.edu/Computer/responsible-use>

Harvey Mudd College
<http://www.hmc.edu/comp/policy/appropriate-use.html>

Indiana University system
<http://www.itpo.iu.edu/policies.html>

University of Georgia
<http://www.uga.edu/compsec/use.html>

University of Southern California
<http://www.usc.edu/Pages/ComputingPolicy.html>

"Issues in Computer Ethics and Social Implications of Computing"
<http://bones.cs.wcupa.edu/~epstein/social.html>

"Cybercitizen Awareness Program"
<http://www.cybercitizenship.org>

A major ethical issue for students, researchers, and writers is the use of copyrighted sources. For this reason, we devote an entire section of this chapter (3b) to it.

Some of the netiquette conventions described in 3c touch on ethical issues, and we encourage you to read that section to get a better sense of what constitutes responsible use of the Internet.

3b Using copyrighted sources in your work

You are free to access and read any material that is published on the Internet. Whenever you reproduce information found on the Internet, however, you are in fact disseminating that information and thus may need to seek permission to use it. Material that is copyrighted often includes a notice with the word *copyright*, the symbol ©, and the name of the copyright holder:

> Copyright © 1995–1997 by Benedict O'Mahoney. All rights reserved.

Such a notice indicates that the material is protected by copyright and that unauthorized use is illegal. However, even material that doesn't include a notice is likely to be copyrighted. Asssume material is copyrighted unless you know it is not.

Be aware that anyone—instructors included—can use today's fast **search tools** to detect plagiarism by searching the Web for texts containing identifiable strings of words from the document in question. In addition, many graphics now contain **digital watermarks** that enable Web managers to trace the unauthorized use of copyrighted images. To avoid embarrassment and more serious consequences of plagiarism, make a habit of providing accurate and complete citations for information you find on the Web.

1 Requesting permission to use copyrighted sources

If you want to reproduce a large part or all of the content of a copyrighted source, then you need to write to the

```
FROM: stumiller@acs.eku.edu
TO:    comments@benedict.com
SENT: Monday, January 10, 2000
CC:    stumiller@acs.eku.edu
SUBJ: Request for permission

Dear Benedict O'Mahoney,

I wish to request permission to quote from
"Copyright Fundamentals" on _The Copyright
Website._ Quotations from your text will
appear in a research paper to be submitted
in my webfolio (collection of online
writings). The paper will, in part, help
writers do research on the Internet. I
will, of course, give credit to you as
the author of my source and will specify
<www.benedict.com/fund.htm#fund> as the
original URL. Please let me know if such
permission is granted. Thank you.

Alice Miller <stumiller@acs.eku.edu>
```

Figure 3.1
Sample request for permission to quote from a source

copyright holder and request permission to use the desired text, image, or file. Figures 3.1 and 3.2 demonstrate how one might ask for permission to reproduce a copyrighted text and a graphic to be used as an illustration.

If permission is granted, then you may use the source as you have indicated. If permission is denied, however, you must respect the denial. You may, of course, create a **hyperlink** to the source itself, refer to the source, or paraphrase or summarize its contents, citing the source appropriately.

In an educational, noncommercial setting, "fair use" of copyrighted materials is allowed. Fair-use provisions in copyright law usually designate some copying as legal. The intent is to increase public access to the work without infringing on the benefits derived from the work by the author or publisher. Generally, fair use of copyrighted material for personal, noncommercial use is not a copyright infringement.

Laws regarding rights to intellectual property available on the Internet continue to evolve. If you need answers to questions about copyright law, permissions,

FROM: stumiller@acs.eku.edu
TO: malick@www.acm.uiuc.edu
SENT: Tuesday, January 11, 2000
CC: stumiller@acs.eku.edu
SUBJ: Request for permission

Dear _____,

I am a student at Eastern Kentucky
University. I would like to request permission to download and use <escher-2worlds.gif>
as an illustration of M. C. Escher's work.
The illustration will be part of a class project for my first-year composition course.
When using the image, I will cite <http://
www.acm.uiuc.edu:80/rml/Gifs/Escher> as the
URL, unless you specify a different credit
line. Thank you for considering my request.

Alice Miller <stumiller@acs.eku.edu>

Figure 3.2
Sample request for permission to download and use an image

and good ethical practice, turn to the Internet for up-to-
date information on these subjects. The sites listed in
Box 3.2 provide useful information.

2 Avoiding plagiarism by acknowledging online sources

Plagiarism, defined as the fraudulent presentation of
someone else's work as your own, is almost universally

Box 3.2
Sites providing information on copyright issues

United States Copyright Office
<http://www.loc.gov/copyright>
Copyright Clearance Center: Permissions Made Easy
<http://www.copyright.com/default.asp>
Copyright and Fair Use
<http://fairuse.stanford.edu/>
Copyright Management Center
<http://www.copyright.iupui.edu>
The Copyright Website
<http://www.benedict.com>

condemned. Nearly all style manuals explain why plagiarism must be avoided and how to give credit to other writers when citing their ideas or wording. Moreover, most colleges and universities have official policies concerning plagiarism and specific penalties for punishing offenders. (See, for example, the "Carnegie Mellon University Policy on Cheating and Plagiarism" at <http://www.cmu.edu/policies/documents/Cheating.html>.)

The Internet makes it easy for you to use other sources in your writing and encourages collaboration among its users. As a result, the traditional notion of the "author"as a single individual working alone on his or her document can be difficult to maintain in an online context. Many software programs promote group writing in the form of collaborative drafting, editing, and revision. Such "patchwriting" means that our print-based notions about who "owns" a text—and what exactly constitutes an *author*—must now be rethought and perhaps redefined.[1]

The fifth edition of the *MLA Handbook for Writers of Research Papers* by Joseph Gibaldi (Modern Language Association, 1999) recognizes that certain forms of writing often involve collaborative efforts, which the traditional guidelines regarding plagiarism do not always address:

> [One] issue concerns collaborative work, such as a group project you carry out with other students. Joint participation in research and writing is common and, in fact, encouraged in many courses and in many professions, and it does not constitute plagiarism provided that credit is given for all contributions. One way to give credit, if roles were clearly demarcated or were unequal, is to state exactly who did what. Another way, especially if roles and contributions were merged and truly shared, is to acknowledge all concerned equally. Ask your instructor for advice if you are not certain how to acknowledge collaboration. (33–34)

Authors of print sources commonly acknowledge participants in collaborative writing projects at the beginning of a book, essay, or research report, often in a preface or note. Internet writers, too, must acknowledge

---

[1] See, for example, Rebecca Howard, *Standing in the Shadow of Giants: Plagiarists, Authors, Collaborators* (Norwood: Ablex, 1999).

help from other authors and researchers, as well as from page designers, graphic artists, funding institutions, and software developers. In your hypertext document, you can dedicate a separate linked page to acknowledging help and sources. Figure 3.3 shows an extract from a typical acknowledgments page.

When you engage in online composition and publication, not only do you open yourself to the possibilities of collaboration, you also assume responsibility for acknowledging the influences that make such writing possible.

Acknowledgments

Project Censored Canada (PCC) is very much a collective effort. We wish to thank the journalists who wrote the underreported stories; the magazines and newspapers that published them; and the journalists, activists, and other interested individuals who nominated the stories. We also wish to thank the researchers, students participating in PCC seminars at both Simon Fraser University and the University of Windsor in the spring of 1995. Our researchers analyzed approximately 150 nominations to determine if they qualified as underreported stories and then selected the top eighteen for forwarding to our distinguished national panel of judges, to whom thanks are also due.

Student Researchers

Diane Burgess, Laurie Dawkins, Cameron Dempsey, Chantal Ducoeurjoly, Bill Duvall, James Duvall, Shoni Field, David Fittler, Rita Fromholt, Tony Fusaro, Dale Gamble, Madelaine Halls, Clayton Jones, Ava Lew, Cheryl Linstead, Kirsten Madsen, Lauren Maris, Jennifer Morrison, Carmen Pon, Elizabeth Rains, Steve Rennie, Humaira Shah, Karen Whale, and Tracy Workman.

Figure 3.3
Sample acknowledgments page

"Project Censored Canada: Researching the Nation's News Agenda. A joint project of the School of Communication, Simon Fraser University Department of Communication Studies, University of Windsor," 25 Apr. 1996, 26 June 1996 <http://cc6140mac.comm.sfu.ca /acknowledgements.html>.

3 Citing Internet sources in hypertext essays

A **hypertext** essay often contains links to sources cited in the text. For this reason, some instructors do not require their students to append a list of works cited when they are citing only Internet sources in an essay. If all of the sources are already connected to the **HTML** text, readers can retrieve them without a separate list.

Since Internet sites can easily be revised, archived, or even removed from the Internet, some instructors require a list of sources even for a hypertext essay citing only Internet sources. Such a list provides a handy summary of all the Internet sources used in the essay and demonstrates the nature and extent of the author's research. If you are required to provide a list of Internet works cited, see Chapters 5–8 for guidance for citing and documenting Internet sources. You are never wrong to include a list of works cited; if you're not sure of your instructor's requirements, provide such a list.

3c Observing netiquette

Netiquette (a combination of the words *net* and *etiquette*) refers to the courtesies that responsible Internet users extend to each other.

Not all Internet forums observe the same forms of netiquette; the expectations of your audience will determine what is acceptable. For example, when using **email** or **real-time communication**, you may sometimes write informally, overlooking some conventions of spelling, punctuation, and mechanics. Documents published on the **Web** are, by contrast, perceived as more public and permanent than email or **listserv** postings and therefore require more attention to writing conventions. In particular, readers in academic communities expect Web writers to observe all the conventions of essay and research paper writing.

The following two rules of thumb apply to all Internet publications: (1) respect your readers, and (2) respect others' time.

Respect your readers. People from all over the world communicate on the Internet. In your writing, you must often consider the needs and reactions of global audiences. Don't assume, for example, that slang, jargon, and abbreviations will be understood by everyone.

Explain ideas carefully and provide contexts to help others follow and understand your points. If you disagree with someone publicly online, do so tactfully. If you must disagree strongly with someone, consider doing so by private correspondence. Don't engage in **flaming** (the public posting of personal attacks). Readers on listservs and in newsgroups find such posting offensive.

Respect others' time. Remember that your readers value their time. When using email, make your messages easy to read and answer. For Web audiences, design your documents so that they can be downloaded quickly. When communicating in real time, use commonly known abbreviations and acronyms. Whenever you communicate via the Internet, do all you can to help others and yourself save time when reading, responding, or downloading.

For general introductions to netiquette, read the following guides:

"The Core Rules of Netiquette"
<http://www.albion.com/netiquette/corerules.html>

"Understanding and Using the Internet: Beginners Guide"
<http://www.pbs.org/uti/guide/netiquette.html>

1 The World Wide Web

The **World Wide Web** connects a multitude of Internet resources by **hypertext**. Using **HTML (hypertext markup language)**, Web writers publish pages, often enhanced by graphics or audio, that typically include links to other Web pages or sites. When you publish research papers or other writing on the Web, make a point of observing the following guidelines.

Avoid plagiarism by acknowledging your Web sources. Avoid plagiarism by clearly indicating both print and online sources for borrowed ideas, direct quotations, paraphrases, and summaries in your print or online texts. See 3b and Chapters 5–8 for specific advice on citing and documenting Internet sources.

Notify Web-site owners when you make links to their Web pages. Although you're not required to ask permission to link to another's site, most Web-page authors appreciate a brief email message stating that you intend to create a link to their Web sites. Doing so

```
FROM: linda@kahana.pgd.hawaii.edu
TO:   engharnack@acs.eku.edu,
      phiklepp@acs.eku.edu
SENT: Thursday, January 6, 2000
CC:   gjtaylor@kahana.pgd.hawaii.edu
SUBJ: Request to link citation guidelines
```

Dear Dr. Harnack and Dr. Kleppinger,

Jeff Taylor and I have released a new educational Web journal called _Planetary Science Research Discoveries_. It is a monthly publication written for teachers and students. Your essay "Beyond the MLA Handbook: Documenting Electronic Sources on the Internet" at <http://english.ttu.edu/kairos/1.2/inbox/mla.html> is a very helpful document, and we would like to link it to our site at <http://www.soest.hawaii.edu/PSRdiscoveries>. May we have your permission to do so? Thank you very much.

Linda Martel
Education Specialist—Planetary Geosciences
University of Hawaii
linda@kahana.pgd.hawaii.edu

Figure 3.4
Sample request for permission to link to another site

helps them gauge the nature of their audience and the significance of their work, and gives them the opportunity to provide additional information. Figure 3.4 shows how such a request might be worded.

Remember the value of your viewers' time. For Web users who view documents with modems, downloading images can be time-consuming. Instead of placing very large images in HTML documents, limit the file size of the image to 20 kilobytes (KB) or create **thumbnails** (miniature images) that viewers can click on to see an enlarged version. (See 9e for more detailed advice.) When appropriate, describe file sizes when providing links. For example, if you include video, sound, or large graphics files with your text, indicate file sizes next to any file names or descriptive information (e.g., Juan Gris, *Portrait of Picasso*, 160 KB). Your readers can then estimate how long it will take to download the file.

Include the option of text-only links in your HTML documents. Not all Internet users desire or benefit from graphics. Some readers skip graphics to save research time. Others, lacking a graphic browser, are not able to view documents containing an **image map** but no text. Moreover, the visually impaired regularly "view" documents with devices that can read text to them. For these audiences, provide text-only options in your HTML documents. See "The Lynx Manifesto" at <http://world.std.com/~adamg/manifesto.html> for tips on constructing texts that describe images for users whose browsers don't display them.

Indicate the date of last revision. Include the date of your last revision (preferably at the end of the document) so readers can gauge the currency of your publication.

Keep URLs as simple as possible. Because URLs are often long or case-sensitive, readers sometimes find them difficult to copy exactly. Keep file names and directory paths simple; use capital letters sparingly.

Provide URL information in your Web text. Not all browsers automatically provide a document's URL somewhere on the printout. It will be very helpful to readers if you include the actual URL in the document itself, preferably after the date of publication or last revision. Readers of printouts will then be able to refer to your document's URL accurately and access its Web site.

Give readers a way to contact you. Near the end of your publication, give readers the opportunity to send you an email message by providing a link to your own email address.

Protect your work. Any original work created after 1978 automatically has copyright protection. However, it is good practice to protect the integrity of your Web publications with a copyright notice that includes the word *Copyright* or the symbol ©, the year of publication or creation, and the copyright holder's name, as in the following example:

▶ © 1997 Donna Hawkins

To establish a more defensible copyright for legal purposes, register your work with the U.S. Copyright

Office, which offers forms and further information at <http://www.loc.gov/copyright>.

Be aware of legal issues. Writers who misuse copyrighted materials or publish obscene, harassing, or threatening materials on the Internet can violate local, state, national, or international laws and be subject to litigation. As a writer and publisher of electronic documents, you are responsible for what you allow users worldwide to access. See 3a for a discussion of online ethics and 3d for information about safety issues.

For more on Web netiquette, see Arlene Rinaldi's "The Net: User Guidelines and Netiquette" at <http://www.fau.edu/netiquette/net>.

2 Email

Email (electronic mail) lets you exchange messages with others via the Internet. To your **ASCII** messages, you can attach formatted text files as well as files containing audio and graphics. When sending email, remember that its content is harder to keep private than that of **snailmail**. You can make an online communication secure by encryption (coding), but once your recipients decode it, they might, even accidentally, forward it to anyone else on the Internet. Treat every email message, even so-called private ones, as potentially public information. Although you may consider it improper, by hitting the Forward command your recipient can send your message (or part of it) to individuals, newsgroups, or listservs. Govern your use of email accordingly.

The following are widely practiced guidelines for email netiquette. (For general information about email, see 2c.)

Think before emailing. Don't email strangers—experts, others, even your instructors—for information about a topic until you have tried finding out answers to your questions on your own. If you do end up emailing them, they will appreciate the fact that you already have a basic understanding of the issue you are researching.

Address email carefully. Email addresses are sometimes difficult to type exactly (e.g., the letter O is easily confused with the number 0). When sending email, enter the address with special care. If you type the address incorrectly, an "undeliverable mail" notice may not appear in your mailbox for a while, and you may not realize your error until hours or days later. The best ways to ensure accuracy are to use your address book, to copy and paste an address from a previous message, or, if responding, to use the Reply function.

Provide useful subject lines.   All email messages are delivered with **subject lines** (brief descriptions that appear in the recipient's email directory). Your subject line should provide a short description of your message's content or main point. Some readers receive many messages daily, so get your recipient's attention by making sure the subject line accurately reflects your message's content:

▶   Subject: ENG 101 MOO Schedule

While your readers may be satisfied with short descriptions of content, they may also appreciate the use of the following notices when appropriate.

Nonurgent information: If your message doesn't require a response, type "FYI:" (For Your Information:) at the beginning of the subject line:

▶   Subject: FYI: Florida Tour Travel Schedule

Time-sensitive information: When sending information that requires a quick response, use "URGENT:"

▶   Subject: URGENT: What about Florida tour?

Long messages: If the message is long, warn readers with a parenthetical notice:

▶   Subject: Complete FL Itinerary (LONG)

When replying to or forwarding a message, change the subject line if necessary.   If you change the topic when you're replying to or forwarding a message, rephrase the subject line to reflect the change in your message's content or your purpose in sending it.

Write crisp, clear messages.   Write crisply and to the point. Avoid overly long sentences. In general, make your online paragraphs shorter than those you would write for an offline medium. Skip a line between paragraphs (rather than indenting them) to make your messages easier to read. Use numbered lists when possible. When quoting from a previous message, quote only what is necessary.

Use well-known abbreviations.   Many online correspondents use abbreviations and acronyms in informal email (and other informal messages). Box 3.3 lists some abbreviations that are generally acceptable in informal writing.

Use normal capitalization.   Don't send messages using all capital letters. Capitalized text is harder to read than lowercase or mixed-case text. In addition, messages composed in capital letters are said to "shout" rather than making their point through effective language. Similarly, avoid using all lowercase letters; such text is also hard to read and too informal for most situations.

Box 3.3
Commonly used online abbreviations

afaik	as far as I know
afk	away from keyboard
atm	at the moment
b	be
b4	before
bbiaf	be back in a few minutes
brb	be right back
btw	by the way
c	see
cul	see you later
f2f	face-to-face
focl	falling off the chair laughing
fwd	forward(ed)
hhoj	Ha! Ha! Only joking!
imho	in my humble opinion
irl	in real life
lol	laughing out loud
oic	Oh, I see!
r	are
rotfl	rolling on the floor with laughter
ttyl	talk to you later
u	you
y	why

For an extensive list of abbreviations, see "Internet IRC Chat Abbreviations & Acronyms" at <http://members.lycos.co.uk/sixfour/bobjude/tutor/abbr/irc.html>.

Use underscore marks or asterisks to indicate emphasis.
Since most email is sent and received in **ASCII** unformatted text, you can't use italics or boldface text to show
emphasis. To show that text should be read as *italicized,*
place an underscore mark before and after whatever letters or words might otherwise be italicized. Another
way to show emphasis (but not specifically italics) is by
putting an asterisk before and after the text in question.

▶ Has anyone read _Moby-Dick_ lately?

▶ I have, and it took me a *long* time!

When responding, delete email headers.   If you answer
a message and include that message in your reply, trim
the first message's **header** (routing information) so that
your correspondent doesn't have to read it.

Quote sparingly to establish your reply's context.   If you
include portions of a previous message in your reply,
quote only what is necessary to remind your correspondent what you are responding to. By Internet convention,
lines included from a previous message are preceded
by **greater-than signs (>)**. Some mail editors and news-
readers automatically mark quoted material with > signs
at the left margin. Others require you to do it manually.

Send attachments with care.   Many email systems let
you send **attachments** with your email messages. (See
2c-2.) When sending attachments, observe the following
guidelines:

- Warn your correspondent by email that you're planning to send an attachment, and ask whether he or
  she can accept it. (If not, you can copy and paste
  word-processed material into an email message, provided the material is not long.)

- Tell the recipient what software you used to create
  the attachment, and give any other information that
  will help the recipient open and use the attachment.

- Tell the recipient how big the file is so that he or she
  can download it at a convenient time. (Few things are
  more frustrating than beginning a download only to
  find that it will take longer than expected.)

- Don't send a large file to many people at once. Doing
  so might overload your email system.

Compose useful signature files. Most email programs let you create a **signature (sig) file** that automatically appears at the end of each message you send. It might, for example, contain your full name, your email address, your homepage URL, your affiliation, and information about contacting you offline:

▶ Andrew Harnack <engharnack@acs.eku.edu>

   <http://www.english.eku.edu/harnack>

   Eastern Kentucky University, Richmond, KY 40475

   Phone: (606) 622-2093 / Fax: (606) 622-1020

By including your email address in a sig file, you ensure that readers can reply to you without analyzing the message's header. Keep sig files to four or fewer lines if possible.

Edit and proofread your text. Before sending an email message, review the entire text to make sure it clearly conveys your meaning. (This step is especially important if the text fills more than one screen; by the time you finish writing, you may forget what you wrote in the start of the message.) Ask yourself whether the spontaneity of email has led you to write anything you might later regret. Finally, proofread the text for grammar, spelling, and punctuation errors.

See "Necessary E-Mail Netiquette" at <http://www.stlcc.cc.mo.us/fv/users/rberne/psylecture/manners.htm> for more information.

3 Listservs

Listservs allow people from all over the world who share a common interest to communicate their ideas, ask questions, and develop extensive **threads** on particular topics. (See 2e.) When you join a listserv, you'll receive via email a standard letter of welcome. Thereafter, all messages sent to the group will appear in your email box. You can post messages to everyone on the listserv; you can unsubscribe (sign off) from a list at any time; and you can usually get a list of the listserv's members and their email addresses. Not all listservs are open to the public; subscription to many professional and scholarly lists is by special application. Consult Tile.net at <http://www.tile.net> for an extensive list and description of listservs.

Netiquette for listservs includes all of the guidelines for **email** correspondence (see 3c-2). The following advice extends email netiquette to include specific courtesies that listserv subscribers observe.

Save your letter of confirmation.   After subscribing, save your confirmation letter; it contains important information on how to send messages to the list, how to contact the **listowner**, how to suspend incoming messages if you're away for more than a day or two, and how to unsubscribe from the listserv.

Read the listserv's FAQ.   Most listservs periodically post an **FAQ** document or make one easily available to subscribers. Answers to questions about netiquette are generally included.

Lurk before posting.   After you join a list, monitor the messages for a few days to get a feel for the tone of the conversation and what topics are considered appropriate. Such **lurking** lets you get to know the group before you start posting.

Ask for private responses when appropriate.   Not all messages need go to every listserv subscriber. For example, when conducting a survey, ask that responses be sent to you personally. Once you've gotten answers to your questions (whether as public postings or as private email), post a summary of the answers to the group.

Don't clutter a listserv with well-known information.   If you provide a commonly known answer to someone's question, do so by private email. If someone posts a message that is off the subject, don't reply to the list; instead, reply by email. Private responses help minimize the number of duplicate public responses to a single question.

Delete extraneous text when responding to previous postings.   When quoting another person's message, delete parts that aren't relevant to your reply. For example, never quote an entire long message if all you add is "I agree!" When you quote selectively, be sure not to distort the other person's meaning.

Suspend mail or unsubscribe appropriately.   If you need to suspend mail for a while or unsubscribe from the list-serv altogether, don't send your request to the listserv itself; instead, consult the FAQ or your confirmation letter for directions on how to suspend mail and un-subscribe.

For further discussion, see Arlene Rinaldi's "The Net: User Guidelines and Netiquette: Listservs/Mailing Lists /Discussion Groups" at <http://www.fau.edu/netiquette /net/dis.html>.

4 Newsgroups

Newsgroups allow you to participate online in forums dedicated to specific topics. (See 2f.) You can read mes-sages that people have posted, respond to them, and write and send your own postings. Many of the courte-sies observed by newsgroup participants are similar to those practiced in **email** correspondence and **listserv** participation (see 3c-2 and 3c-3).

Read the newsgroup's FAQ.   If the newsgroup in which you're interested publishes an **FAQ** document, read it carefully. For a list of available newsgroup FAQs, see "FAQs by Newsgroup" at <http://www.faqs.org/faqs /by-newsgroup>.

Lurk before posting.   **Lurk**—that is, read a newsgroup's correspondence—for a while before you post. By lurk-ing, you will get a sense of the participants, their con-cerns, and the communication tone they have estab-lished among themselves.

Ask for private responses when appropriate.   If neither reading a newsgroup's FAQ nor lurking provides the information you need, go ahead and post. If you request basic information, ask that responses be sent to you by email so that other readers don't have to wade through screens full of identical answers.

For more on newsgroup netiquette, see "A Primer on How to Work with the Usenet Community" at <http:// www.use-net.ch/netiquette_engl.html>.

5 Real-time communication

MUDs and MOOs

MUDs (multi-user domains) are **virtual** places that allow many people to communicate in real time. **MOOs (multi-user domains, object-oriented)** permit not only real-time communication but also the creation of virtual objects (e.g., blackboards, quizzes, notebooks, tables and chairs). (See Figure 2.11, on page 53, for an excerpt from a MOO conversation.) Because of MOOs' object-building feature, some instructors and students prefer them to MUDs. Both MUDs and MOOs are widely used in educational settings. Although this section focuses on MOOs, its advice applies to MUDs as well. (See 2g.)

While there are many kinds of MOOs—social, educational, professional, and research-oriented—all MOOs encourage communication that respects other participants and MOO resources. The following netiquette guidelines represent the consensus of people who manage educational MOOs.

Respect other people. Participants in MOOs come from a wide range of cultural, religious, and ethnic backgrounds. Many **newbies** may be apprehensive and will appreciate encouragement and advice. While freedom of speech is valued within MOOs, obscene language, harassment, unwanted sexual advances, and other blatantly offensive behavior and language are not tolerated. Those who engage in such behavior are quickly reprimanded and, if necessary, removed from the MOO.

Familiarize yourself with basic commands. In addition to everyday language, MOOs use a variety of special commands. Before plunging into a MOO conversation, familiarize yourself with the commands of the MOO you're visiting. (For a sampling of MOO commands, visit "Basic MOO Commands" at <http://www.hunter.cuny.edu/ieli/moo-cmd.html>.)

Ask for permission to visit a person or join a conversation. Most people visit a MOO for a specific purpose—perhaps to participate in a class discussion, confer with a teacher, read a chapter from a book, prepare a lecture, work through an assignment, socialize with friends, or work on a project with others. Instead of arriving uninvited in a room where others are present, always "knock on the door" by typing *@knock* and ask if you may join those present by typing *@join*.

Use well-known abbreviations in conversation. MOO conversationalists have created many abbreviations and acronyms useful in real-time communication. Box 3.3 (on page 78) lists some abbreviations used in MOO sessions and in other forms of online communication.

Avoid spamming, spoofing, and spying. To **spam** is to fill another's screen with unwanted text. To *spoof* is to display text that is not obviously attributed to you or your character. To *spy* is to **lurk** for a malicious purpose or use any mechanism that intercepts messages not intended for you. These behaviors violate the standards of courtesy expected among MOOers.

Ask for permission to record conversations. Before recording a MOO session, obtain the permission of all other participants in that session. If you plan to distribute a transcript of a conversation by email (on a distribution list or a **listserv**), announce your intention to do so and get everyone's permission.

Respect the property of others. MOOs contain **virtual** objects (e.g., rooms, desks, chairs, blackboards, laboratory equipment, recorders) that have been created and are owned by registered participants. Some, but not all, objects are available for public use. Don't **teleport** (electronically transport) an object without its owner's permission. Always ask for permission to use objects that don't belong to you; when you have finished using the objects, leave them where you found them.

Respect a MOO's resources. When creating objects in a MOO, remember that MOO resources are limited. Poorly designed objects can affect the performance of the entire MOO. Avoid designing code or creating objects that consume large amounts of processing time or resources. Always consult your MOO's **wizard**, manager, or administrator before starting an extensive project. When copying or modifying someone else's code, ask permission first, and then comply with any requests that person has regarding the use of the code.

For further information about MUDs and MOOs, visit "Educational MUDs and MOOs" at <http://www-ts

.cs.oberlin.edu/rooms/edmoos.html>. For more on MOO netiquette, visit "Collected MOO Manner Guidelines" at <http://www.tengrrl.com/tens/manners.shtml> and "Expected Behavior and Manners for Diversity University MOO" at <http://moo.du.org /dumoo/manners.htm>.

Internet relay chat

Internet relay chat (IRC) is a multi-user, multichannel network that allows people all over the Internet to talk to one another in real time. Each IRC user or "client" chooses a nickname. Topics of discussion on IRC are as varied as the topics of **newsgroups**. Technical and political discussions are popular, especially when world events are unfolding. Most conversations are in English, but there are channels in Finnish, French, German, Japanese, and other languages.

The following advice describes basic IRC netiquette.

Enter and exit conversations unobtrusively. You don't need to greet everybody on a channel personally; one "Hello!" or its equivalent is usually enough. Don't expect everyone to return your greeting. If you must say hello or goodbye to someone you know, do it in a private message.

Be patient. Instead of jumping headfirst into a conversation, **lurk** a while to get a feel for the tone of the conversation and the personalities of participants. When you do start chatting, realize you'll need to be on the same channel for quite a while (maybe several days) before others recognize you as a "regular."

Use well-known abbreviations in chats. Participants in IRC often use abbreviations to speed up communication. See Box 3.3 (on page 78) for a list of commonly used abbreviations. "Shano's Chat Acronym Database" at <http://www.shano.com/acronym> provides an extensive list of IRC abbreviations and acronyms.

For more information about IRC, consult the following Web documents:

"A Short IRC Primer"
<http://www.irchelp.org/irchelp/ircprimer.html>

"Internet Relay Chat FAQ"
<http://www.irchelp.org/irchelp/altircfaq.html>

"Yahoo! Computers and Internet : Internet : Chats and Forums : Internet Relay Chat (IRC)"

<http://dir.yahoo.com/Computers_and_Internet
/internet/chats_and_forums/internet_relay_chat_irc_>

3d Using the Internet safely

Like frontier societies of yore, the Internet is largely unregulated, so you need to take certain steps to protect your privacy and personal safety. By following the commonsense precautions outlined in this section, you can keep undesirable consequences of your Internet use to a minimum.

1 Protecting your privacy

Guarding your identity When you visit the Internet, your computer sends requests for documents with a unique identification code—usually an **IP (Internet protocol) number**—so that **servers** can return the documents to you. Similarly, your **email** address is embedded in messages that you send, and recipients need that information in order to reply. These forms of identification are generally helpful and desirable, but you may find yourself in situations where you wish to hide your identity. In these cases, use a privacy service such as Anonymizer at <http://www.anonymizer.com>.

In chat rooms, **MOOs**, and other discussion areas on the Internet, your messages to others are usually labeled with your "screen name" (which may also be called a **username**, *nickname, character name, avatar, alias,* or *handle*). Many sites let you choose your own screen name, and most will help you connect that screen name with a list of your interests and hobbies so that other users with similar interests can contact you. Remember that the information conveyed by screen names (such as "chicagobobby") and related personal data are not reliable; the person represented by the screen name may be pretending to be of a different age, race, gender, and so on, or to have a personality very different from his or her real one. To protect yourself from unwanted personal contact and potential abuse, adhere to the following guidelines for sharing personal information on the Internet:

• Use your full (real) name only in safe situations (e.g., sending email to recipients you know, chatting with classmates, or communicating with businesses or other well-known organizations).

- Never reveal your home address or telephone number in chat rooms or other public areas, and be very cautious about distributing that information through email or on your own Web pages.

- Be cautious when describing your age, location, or physical appearance over the Internet, because a chat companion (for example) might be able to use that information in unexpected ways.

To learn more about safeguarding your Internet identity, visit SafeKids.Com <http:// www.safekids.com> and Software to Protect Children <http://www.psychpage.com /family/soft.html>. While these sites emphasize children's needs, their principles for Internet security also apply to adult users.

Controlling cookies Many Web sites attempt to use **cookies** to save information about your visit. Stored on your personal computer as a short text file, a cookie gives a Web site data about any previous visit(s) you've made to that site. For example, a catalog merchandiser can record the sizes and colors of items you purchase, and then suggest those options to you on your next visit.

If you'd rather not provide such information, disable cookies by resetting your **browser**'s preferences. In Netscape Communicator, open the Edit menu, select Preferences, and highlight the Advanced category. Then, under the Cookies section, choose from the following options:

- Accept all cookies
- Accept only cookies that get sent back to the originating server
- Disable cookies
- Warn me before accepting a cookie

In Microsoft Internet Explorer, open the View menu, select Internet Options, and click on the Advanced tab. Scroll down to the Cookies section and choose one of the following options:

- Always accept cookies
- Prompt before accepting cookies

- Disable all cookie use

Special programs such as Cookie Pal at <http://www
.kburra.com/cpal.html> and Cookie Protection at <http://
www.hotscripts.com/Detailed/1703.html> enable you to
control the use of cookies as you browse.

Protecting financial information   When buying goods or
making financial transactions over the Internet, always
check the *security indicator* in your browser's **status bar**.
The security indicator tells you whether your communications with the site you are currently visiting are protected by encryption (meaning that the information
being transmitted can be interpreted correctly only by
your computer and the server at the other end). When
you visit a *secure* site, other computers and networks
that help transmit your data cannot decode it to discover sensitive personal information such as credit card or
Social Security numbers.

In Netscape Communicator, the security indicator
looks like a padlock; the lock is "open" when you are
viewing an insecure site and "closed" when you are connected to a secure site. (See Figure 2.1 on page 38.) In
Microsoft Internet Explorer, the security indicator also
looks like a padlock, but it appears only when you connect to a secure site. (See Figure 2.2 on page 39.) When
you have finished your transaction and return to normal
browsing, the security indicator automatically returns to
its normal state.

For more on Internet privacy issues, see The Privacy
Page at <http://www.privacy.org>.

2 Protecting your safety

While your computer itself poses no physical threat to
you, under the following conditions your use of the
Internet could put you at personal risk.

Objectionable Web sites   Perhaps most innocuous are
moments when you unintentionally browse to a site
whose content leaves you uncomfortable, annoyed, or
offended, regardless of how briefly the message or picture is displayed on your screen. For example, you may
be working through a list of search results and unex-
pectedly open a page containing obscenities, or you may
type a URL incorrectly and suddenly see pictures that
offend you. Since there are no restrictions on what peo-

ple may publish on the Internet, such incidents are practically unavoidable. To register a protest, send email to either the page's author or the Web site's system administrator. (The email address for Web system administrators is often <web@system.domain>; for example, <web@eku.edu> would be the appropriate address for concerns about pages associated with Eastern Kentucky University.)

You can decrease the likelihood of encountering objectionable material by surprise—and control what sites children or other users have access to—by installing software that automatically blocks certain sites or types of content. These programs, however, have serious drawbacks; for example, they cannot recognize objectionable content in pictures, and they will block pages that contain innocent uses of their target terms. Alternatively, you can use special software or built-in functions of your browser to filter sites according to their content ratings (see 4c-7), but remember that the rating a page receives, if it is rated at all, is entirely up to the page's author. A third option is to use a "safe" searching tool such as AltaVista's Family Filter <http://www.altavista.com>, Yahooligans! <http://www.yahooligans.com>, or Ask Jeeves for Kids <http://www.ajkids.com>. These search tools promise to screen out objectionable sites so that they don't appear among search results. For more on "safe" Web surfing, visit <http://www.safekids.com>.

Offensive email More ominous than stumbling on offensive material is receiving offensive or threatening email at your personal address. Replying to the sender is usually not the best solution, since doing so may gratify him or her and result in more unwanted email. Instead, send your complaint to the "postmaster" (who is usually a human) at the sender's **domain** address. For example, <postmaster@acs.eku.edu> is the appropriate address for complaints about senders whose addresses end with *@acs.eku.edu*. In your message, include a copy of the offensive email and your comments about it; without your comments, the message might be misinterpreted as your original work! If you send a complaint, don't delete the original message from your computer; its headers may contain information the postmaster needs. Many email postmasters take immediate, decisive action—such as disabling the user's email privileges—

when they receive complaints about messages containing harassing, abusive, or otherwise offensive content. This procedure will not be effective if the sender is using someone else's address (a technique sometimes called *spoofing*), changing email accounts rapidly, or sending messages anonymously. But email messages often contain enough identification information for postmasters and, if necessary, law enforcement personnel to trace their origin to a particular computer used at a particular place and time.

Cyberstalking   The most severe threats to personal safety through Internet activities arise from **cyberstalking** and from injudicious personal meetings. A cyberstalker uses Internet resources maliciously to track a victim's habits and whereabouts. Cyberstalking is a serious crime and must be reported to the authorities as soon as it is discovered. Cyberangels, an organization formed to combat cyberstalking and promote Internet safety, offers help through a "Cyberstalking Online Guide" at <http://www.cyberangels.org/stalking/index.html>.

As you correspond or chat with others on the Internet, you may decide you want to meet in person someone you've never seen. Because it is so easy to disguise oneself during Internet communication, meetings with strangers can pose serious risks to your safety. If you do decide to meet a stranger in person, take the following precautions:

- Meet in a public place where you feel comfortable and where other people will be around.
- Bring along a relative or friend.
- Children should consult responsible adults before arranging any meetings.

Visit SafeKids.Com <http://www.safekids.com> and Software to Protect Children <http://www.psychpage.com/family/soft.html> for more information about Internet safety.

Although the risks described in this section are real, don't let them discourage you from discovering the wealth of valuable information the Internet offers. Chapter 4 helps you find the information you need and evaluate its quality.

CHAPTER FOUR

Choosing and Evaluating Internet Sources

While **Internet** sources can be informative and valuable, they should generally complement information from traditional print sources, not replace print sources entirely. Printed materials (e.g., books, encyclopedias, journals, newspaper articles, pamphlets, brochures, and government publications) are indispensable sources for research on most topics. Unless you are instructed otherwise, use both print and Internet sources in any writing project that requires research. This chapter looks at issues you are likely to encounter when doing research on the Internet.

4a   Using Internet sources in your writing

Calling your readers' attention to Internet sources in your writing can give your work a special flair and distinction. However, if you use Internet sources, you must be careful to evaluate and cite them properly. When using and documenting Internet sources, follow three basic principles:

1. In your writing, make clear to readers which source you are referring to and how you understand its relevance to your topic.
2. Whatever citation style you use (MLA, APA, *Chicago*, CBE, or another style), give your readers enough information to enable them to retrieve the source material if possible.
3. In your research notes or portfolio, store the data you collect about your Internet sources. Whether you store your notes and portfolio materials electronically, on paper, or both, you must preserve accurate data about your accessing of Internet sources. If possible, print out your Internet source bibliography whether you are required to or not.

As these three principles emphasize, you should pay careful attention to the details of reference citations. If you want readers to trust what you write, you must give them enough information to enable them to review your sources. Citing Internet sources is especially challenging because the Internet itself is constantly changing. New and different modes of access appear so frequently that pre-Internet documentation methods are often inadequate.

As information technology develops, new documentation conventions are needed. Chapters 5–8 of this book explain how to document online sources. For the latest information about citation, visit the **World Wide Web** site for *Online!* at <http://www.bedfordstmartins.com/online>. If you have a question about your research, difficulty documenting a source, or trouble locating information, email us. We'll do all we can to help you find answers and solutions.

4b Identifying useful Internet sources

Finding sources of information on the Internet is relatively easy, but evaluating their quality requires great care. Searching the Internet with a tool such as Yahoo! or AltaVista, you're likely to get a list of potential sources whose quality and relevance varies greatly. The fact that a source is listed in a **subject directory**, linked to another Web page, or mentioned in an advertisement does not guarantee that it is reliable.

Deciding which Internet sources are most valuable for your project requires patience and practice because there are few, if any, standards regarding what may be published on the Web. Some computer system administrators and government agencies may try to restrict access to material they deem offensive. But such regulations, even if they could be enforced, would have no impact on the *truth* or *clarity* of claims expressed on the Internet.

Consider this: not only is there no editorial board for most Internet publications, there also is no market force to drive incompetent or untrustworthy publications off the Web. The democracy of the Internet is apparent from a Search Results screen, where each **hit** appears as important as all the rest.

Confronted by such anarchy, but knowing that *some* Internet information is reputable, you as a careful researcher should evaluate Internet sources by asking questions like these:

- Which sources are worth inspecting?
- What information is available about a given document?
- How can I evaluate the reliability of a source?
- How should I represent my evaluation in my writing?

This section offers help with answering the first question, and sections 4c–e provide guidance for answering the other three.

The menus you generate by searching with the Internet tools discussed in 1g often stretch to many screens and include hundreds or thousands of items. The relevance of some items on the list may be obscure because the terms you searched for are located somewhere in the document's text and are not yet visible on your screen. After you open a document you can, of course, use your **browser**'s Find function (usually on the Edit menu) to see where in the text your **keywords** actually appear. Only as you examine the document can you begin to evaluate its usefulness and integrity.

Once you have a list of search results, create an entry on your **bookmark list** for the results screen so you can return to it easily. As you review the results, create additional **bookmarks** for useful-looking sites and documents. (See 4c-1 for more on bookmarks.)

As you make preliminary selections of interesting sources, use the reliability standards discussed in 4d to help you limit the field. For example, a document may seem to be strongly supportive of your position, but if you can't identify its author or sponsoring organization, the material is not worth further consideration. Once you learn to recognize the telltale marks of worthwhile sites, you'll find it easy to sort out the most promising sources even from very long lists of search results. Potentially valuable Web sources are signaled by the following criteria:

- Clear authorship or sponsorship (if the latter, preferably by an organization you recognize)

- A clear connection between the author or sponsor and your topic

- A clear presentation of facts and opinions, with care taken to avoid errors in grammar, spelling, and structure

- Screen layouts and graphics (where necessary) that enhance the information and facilitate navigation

- Citations of other sources, where relevant, giving details you can check

- Updated links that lead to other high-quality sites

4c Gathering information about your Internet sources

Once you have assembled a list of useful sources, the next step is to gather the information you'll need to use the source. Capturing this information immediately is vital for finding it again and will make it easier to cite the source in your writing. Because Internet documents lack covers, dust jackets, and title pages, you'll have to inspect a source carefully for the information you need. Box 4.1 lists the types of information you should record.

Remember to *print out* backup copies of information you are storing electronically. Then, if a disaster strikes your electronic data, you will still be able to complete your project.

Box 4.1
Information to record about an Internet source

Author(s)

Title of document

Electronic address

Date of publication

Date of access

Part or section heading or number

Other important information (e.g., type of email message)

---

1 **Recording and bookmarking the information you collect**

When working with print documents, you may be in the habit of recording essential bibliographic data either by hand or by photocopy. For Web sources, much of the information you need is readily available while you are viewing a file, either on the screen or through browser menu selections. As you find useful sources on the Internet, develop the twin habits of (1) recording the document information for future reference, and (2) making a browser **bookmark** so that you can easily return to the source.

Recording the document information page   Printing the first page of text from a Web document usually captures the page's title, its URL, and your date of access. In general, don't print the whole text of long Web documents. For passages you intend to quote or paraphrase, open a word-processor window and use the copy-and-paste method to put the data into a file. Then print out this file's contents. If you are using Netscape Communicator, you can open the Page Info window—from the View menu—to record a page's URL and its last modification date. (You can see such a window in Figure 4.4 on page 102.) Because a document's URL is crucial for your work, you must record it with absolute accuracy; therefore, any electronic means of storage or printing is preferable to handwriting. Be sure to record the date you access each URL. (See 4c-4 for help with finding URLs.)

Depending on the programs you use, you may be able to save important Web pages to files on your computer, archiving their information as you obtained it. On your browser's File menu, select "Save As" and follow the prompts. Alternatively, you can save the text from the page by opening a word-processor window and using the copy-and-paste method to put the data into a file. If the page includes graphics you want to keep, you must save each graphic separately by **right-clicking** over it and selecting "Save Image As."

Bookmarking the Web site   When you find a useful Web site, add a **bookmark** immediately. If you follow this practice, your bookmark list will grow into a complete index of your Internet sources, automatically recording much of the information you need for documentation. Your browser's menus give you access to the bookmarks file, which you can examine to find a source's title, its URL, and the date you accessed the bookmark.

If you share a computer with other users, your ability to make bookmarks may be limited, or you may worry that others will erase your bookmarks. Many graphic browsers let you save bookmarks from your current Web search to a file and later import them to the browser again. If so, you can carry your bookmarks on a floppy disk for security. Another, less convenient method is to use the copy-and-paste method to transfer URLs between your browser's screen and a text file in your computer.

2 Locating the correct title for a document

The most appropriate title for an Internet document is not always the heading that first gets your attention on the screen. Browsers show the document's actual title at the top of the screen window. If the onscreen title is obviously incomplete, or if you have doubts about its accuracy, look for the complete version in Netscape Communicator's Page Info window (which you can access from the View menu) or in Microsoft Internet Explorer's Properties window (which you can access from the Context menu with a click of the right mouse button). If the window title is uninformative or otherwise unsuitable, select the first main heading on the Web page.

Some documents are listed by search tools with the designation "no title" or with only a URL. If a document doesn't have a title, you will need to provide one so that you can find the document easily on your bookmark list and also cite it properly later. Avoid using "no title" and similar designations as titles of documents; instead, follow these rules of thumb:

• *If the untitled document contains text,* construct an appropriate title from the first major heading or the first text line. Enclose the title in square brackets to show that it is your editorial construction.

• *If the untitled document is a graphic,* construct a descriptive title such as "Photograph of Albert Einstein" and enclose it in square brackets.

• *If the untitled document is part of a larger hypertext work* (e.g., a chapter in a story), record the title of the complete work and then refer to the untitled source by its text division. Use this method when a source's URL contains a number sign (#), as in <http://www.pinerest.org/gnrlinfo.htm#MISSIONSTATEMENT>, the Mission Statement section of Pine Rest Christian Mental Health Services' General Info page.

3 Looking for the author(s) of a document

Authors of Internet documents don't always make their names readily visible. If the name of the person or organization responsible for an Internet source is not stated clearly at the beginning or end of the document, try the following approaches before labeling the source "anonymous":

• *Seek a broader context.* If the document has links to related pages at the same site, it may be part of an author's larger collection. You can also use a document's URL to try to locate additional pages by the same author or organization. To do so, delete the last (rightmost) segment of the address in the location bar—back to a slash—and press Enter; this makes your browser ask for files at the next higher Web directory level. For example, if the page at <http://www

.server.net/docs/page.htm> has no author, try the
address <http://www.server.net/docs>.

- *Look for the author's email address.* If the address is not
  clearly visible, use your browser's Find or Search
  function to locate the **@** symbol (which appears in
  every Internet email address).

- *Open the document's source information window,* which
  you access from the View or Context menu in a
  graphic browser. Look for lines that specify the
  "owner" of the document, and record any names or
  email addresses you find.

- *If you locate an email address but no personal name,* try to
  find the real name by "fingering" the address. *Finger*
  is an Internet function that may be available from your
  system prompt (if you have a **terminal connection** to
  the Internet), from software on your own computer, or
  through a Web site such as <http://www.cs.indiana
  .edu/finger>. Finger and similar tools let you match
  names with email addresses. For more information
  about using finger, see Finger! at <http://www.email
  man.com/finger>. While the information from finger
  and other such tools is generally reliable, remember
  that some Internet-connected systems don't respond
  to finger requests and some systems use email
  addresses that won't work with these search tools.

4 Finding a document's URL

Every Internet document has a unique "address," or
URL (uniform resource locator) , which specifies how
the document can be retrieved. Graphic browsers usually display the current URL in a window. Some printer
settings let you record the URL on each printed page
of text. But the easiest way to find and record a document's URL is to use your browser's **bookmark** feature
(described in 2b and 4c-1). Use the URL recorded with
your bookmark unless you decide to shorten it (see the
following section, "Shortening URLS").

The URL for a **telnet** session can't be captured
through your browser's bookmark menu, but you can
record it by opening the **context menu** (e.g., by **right-
clicking** the right mouse button) for the telnet link and
selecting "Add Bookmark."

Shortening URLs In a URL, any material following #
(the number sign) represents a section or division of a
single file. If you're producing printed text and want to
minimize the number of long URLs you show in the text,
you can shorten a URL by ending it at the # sign and
using the section label as a text division (as you would
the page number of a printed book). For example, the
URL

▶ `<http://www.pinerest.org/gnrlinfo.htm#HISTORY>`

can be simplified to

▶ `<http://www.pinerest.org/gnrlinfo.htm>`

if you tell your readers that you're referring to the
HISTORY section of this document.

Very complicated or long URLs can often be avoided
in printed text by citing a preliminary page and explaining briefly how to reach the target. For example, URLs
for search results screens are usually long and uninformative. If, instead of showing the URL <http:/www
.altavista.com/cgi-bin/query?pg=q&kl=XX&stype
=stext&q=%221Mount+Everest%22>, you refer to "the
results of searching for 'Mount Everest' at AltaVista
<http://www.altavista.com>," your readers will readily
be able to retrieve the results themselves.

Typing URLs For rules about typing URLs, see 1d-2.

5 Working with frames

Many Web pages contain two or more **frames**. Frames
let you see and work with several documents in one
screen window. For example, a page might show the
table of contents for a book in one frame and the text in
another frame. Selecting a link in one frame sometimes
changes the display in another frame, but the window,
title, and general layout usually remain unchanged.
Figure 4.1 shows a page with five frames.

Most frames are easily recognized by scroll bars at the
frames' edges that give you control over what you see.
In other cases, the best evidence that you're working
with frames is that the URL in the dialog box remains
unchanged as you click links and watch new information appear in various regions of the window. (If a link

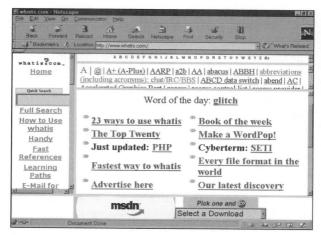

Figure 4.1
A page containing five frames, four of which have scroll bars
<http://www.whatis.com>

inside a frame leads you to a different site or a different part of the same site, the URL will of course change.)

You need to know about frames in order to

- Print what you see in a frame
- Create bookmarks for frames
- Refer accurately to framed information

Printing a frame   To print the information from a frame, you must first make that frame "active" by clicking inside its borders. If you click somewhere else, your printout may not contain what you really wanted.

Bookmarking a frame   Adding bookmarks for pages containing frames can be tricky. Your browser's menu option always records just the main page's URL, ignoring your selections in any frames. To add a Netscape bookmark for the information inside a frame, **right-click** inside the frame and select "Add Bookmark" from the resulting menu. To add an Internet Explorer **favorite** for a frame, open the frame's Context menu (e.g., by right-clicking the mouse in the frame) and select "Add to Favorites." (See Figure 4.2.) When you use such a bookmark, your browser will open it in its own window; that is, you won't see other frames from the original site.

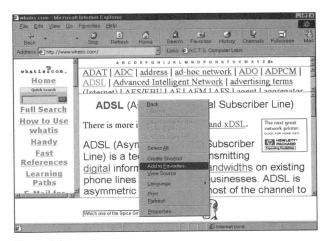

Figure 4.2
Using Microsoft Internet Explorer's context menu to add a favorite
<http://www.whatis.com/adsl.htm>

Referring to information inside a frame   To refer accurately to the information inside a frame, cite the frame like an ordinary Web page (see 5b-1, 6b-1, 7b-1, and 8b-1), using the frame's own URL. The URL displayed in the dialog box gives the address for the whole page you

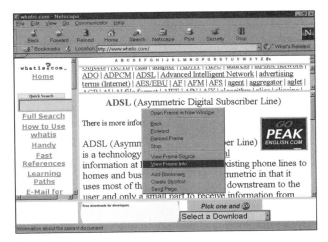

Figure 4.3
Selecting View Frame Info in Netscape Communicator

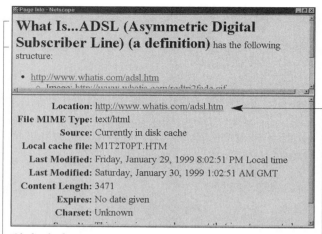

Title for the frame in Figure 4.3   Frame's URL

Figure 4.4
The Frame Info window for the frames indicated in Figure 4.3.
<http://www.whatis.com/adsl.htm>

The right-hand arrow is pointing at the frame's URL, the frame's title is at the top, and the text shows the date this file was last modified.

are viewing; it doesn't point uniquely to any specific frame inside. You can find the active frame's URL from Netscape's Frame Info window (as shown in Figures 4.3 and 4.4). To get the URL from Internet Explorer, open the frame's Context menu and select Properties. (See Figures 4.2 and 4.5.)

6 Keeping track of publication and access dates

Keep track of two dates associated with your Internet sources:

- Publication date (sometimes listed as *revision* or *modification* date)
- Access date

An Internet document's *date of publication* is essential for identifying the document, since a file with a given title can be changed or replaced without a trace. Many

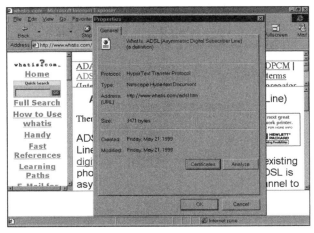

Figure 4.5
A Properties window in Microsoft Internet Explorer
<http://www.whatis.com/adsl.htm>
The date in this window is the date of access, not the date the file was last modified.

Internet authors include a publication date (or a date of *last revision* or *modification*) prominently at the top or bottom of a page.

The *date of access* tells readers when you accessed the document. This date, which usually differs from the publication date, becomes very important when you want to quote from the source or use its data. When you state your access date, you are claiming that the document as reported was available at that particular time. But a document may later be revised or cease to be available. Consider this scenario: you cite a source with a "last revision" date of December 31, 1999. If the author revises the file and simultaneously updates the revision date, others using your citation to locate the file will find a different date and will thus know they're looking at a changed file.

Your browser may provide convenient methods for recording access dates. For example, Netscape Communicator automatically stores the creation and access dates for each bookmark. You can find these dates by opening the Bookmarks menu, selecting Edit Bookmarks, **right-clicking** on a bookmark, and selecting

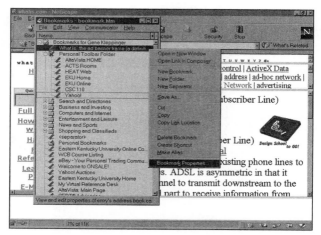

Figure 4.6
Selecting the Bookmark Properties window for a Netscape Communicator bookmark

Bookmark Properties. (See Figure 4.6.) In Microsoft Internet Explorer, you can find the properties for a Favorite by opening the Favorites menu, right-clicking on a favorite, and selecting Properties.

Some **search tools**—notably AltaVista—associate a date with each item found during a search. These dates show how recently the site was indexed by the search tool; again, they do *not* reflect the item's publication date. Always look for the publication date of an Internet source inside the document or on the Document Information page.

Be sure to record a document's publication and access dates as accurately as possible.

7 Understanding site awards and ratings

Many Web sites proudly display logos for awards they have received, including citations such as "Top 5%" or "Best of the Web." Don't let an award logo interfere (positively or negatively) with your judgment of a site's reliability unless you clearly understand the basis for the award. Some logos are sold as promotional gimmicks. Others represent reviews by reputable individuals or organizations, but these judgments often focus primarily on the presentation and organization of the information rather than on its reliability. For example, the International Academy of Digital Arts and Sciences at <http://www.webbyawards.com> sponsors the annual Webby awards, which it deems "*the* preeminent honor for Web sites." The Academy lists six criteria for Webbies: content, structure and navigation, visual design, functionality, interactivity, and overall experience (see <http://www.webbyawards.com/main/webby_awards/criteria.html>). Of these factors, only "content" might measure the reliability of a site's information, but credibility issues are notably absent from the Academy's description of this component:

> *Content:* Content is the information provided on the site. . . . Good content should be engaging, relevant, and appropriate for the audience. You can tell it's been developed for the Web because it's clear and concise and it works in the medium. Good content takes a stand. It has a voice, a point of view. It may be informative, useful, or funny but it always leaves you wanting more.

An award that emphasizes how well a site "works" should not be taken as evidence that the source's content has been evaluated thoroughly.

Several site rating systems have recently been designed to help parents and other authorities cope with growing concerns about obscenity, pornography, and profanity on the Web. The best known of these is the RSACI system, developed by the Recreational Software Advisory Council on the Internet, which defines five levels of intensity in each of four categories (violence, nudity, sex, and language) to describe what a user might encounter at a particular Web site. You can find detailed descriptions for these criteria and their use at <http://www.rsac.org>. Although these ratings may be useful in certain circumstances, their characterization of the moral or psychological orientation of a site's material does not rate the *reliability* of the site's content.

Do not rely on any of the popular ratings schemes to judge the credibility of a site's information. Research efforts such as the Web Credibility Project (see <http://www.webcredibility.org>) hope to reveal details about how people judge the trustworthiness of Web information, which might in turn become the foundation for a content-reliability testing tool. Until these promises can be fulfilled, the best sources for ratings-like information are the annotations provided by some subject directories. For example, INFOMINE at <http://infomine.ucr.edu> lists each Web site's major qualities and "creators" (authors and sponsoring organizations), giving you the basis for judging the likelihood that the site's information is trustworthy. Figure 4.7 shows INFOMINE's detailed annotation for a typical Web site. The Librarian's Index to the Internet at <http://lii.org> also provides helpful evaluative annotations for many Web sites.

4d Evaluating the reliability of an Internet source

Paul Gilster in *Digital Literacy*[1] maintains that "while the Internet offers myriad opportunities for learning, an unconsidered view of its contents can be misleading and deceptive. . . . You cannot work comfortably within this medium until you have established methods for judging the reliability of Web pages, newsgroup postings, and mailing lists" (87). Gilster's point about the necessity of personal involvement—that *you* must become proficient in judging reliability on the Web—cannot be overemphasized. Critical evaluation of Web sources is a daily, unending task *for each user* because the Web's design promotes change and reconstruction—a new link here, a typing error corrected there—which effectively prevents fixed judgments.

But you are not helpless and alone! The Web contains a growing number of documents to help you evaluate the sources you encounter. Links to many of these documents can be found in the subject guide "Evaluation of Information Sources" by Alastair Smith at <http://www.vuw.ac.nz/~agsmith/evaln/evaln .htm>. One of the best summaries of the evaluation process is Elizabeth Kirk's document "Evaluating Information Found

---

[1]Paul Gilster, *Digital Literacy* (New York: Wiley, 1997). See also Paul Gilster, *A Primer on Digital Literacy,* 21 May 1999, Wiley, 29 Sept. 1999 <http://www.rgu.ac.uk/schools/sim/research/netlearn /gilster2.htm>.

Figure 4.7
INFOMINE's detailed annotation of a Web source
<http://infomine.ucr.edu>
The annotation includes a list of site creators and a set of related subjects. The overlaid annotation window appears after clicking "Terms leading to related resources."

on the Internet" at <http://www.library.jhu.edu/elp/useit/evaluate/>. Kirk identifies five major criteria for evaluating all forms of information:

• Authorship
• Publishing body
• Knowledge of other sources
• Accuracy or verifiability
• Currency

The following sections describe these criteria in detail; 4d-6 points to a "checklist" method for carrying out an evaluation, and 4d-7 helps you locate Web site reviews that focus on content evaluation.

1 Authorship

Treat the authorship of an Internet document as the most important factor in evaluating its reliability. Consider these comments from a *New York Times* article about Web information evaluation:

> [E]xperts on Internet research point out that the Web is largely unregulated and unchecked, and so they agree that it is wise to be skeptical: Consider the source. Reconsider the source. Is the information up to date and professional and traceable? Can it be verified, or the source checked, off line? And just who was that source again?[2]

If you cannot see the author's name on a page, follow the suggestions in 4c-3. After determining the names of authors or organizations, make sure that they have authority to speak about your topic. Look for "expert" qualifications on Web pages just as you would in the front matter or dust jackets of printed books. Consider searching for the author's name on the Web or in Usenet. (With AltaVista, for example, you simply type in the author's name and request a Web or Usenet search for text containing information. If the author maintains a homepage, it will be listed.) If biographical links are available, follow them; if the author encourages contact via email, consider the offer seriously. Most Web authors appreciate hearing from people who make use of their information, and the Internet provides a mechanism for responding that most print publications cannot match. An author's homepage may contain helpful information, but comments from others about the author's work are useful as well. Your goal is to establish the author's qualifications for making the claims you want to use.

Here's an example of how to investigate a Web document's authorship. In the **Web discussion forum** message shown in Figure 2.10 (on page 50), the author's name is given simply as "Dan M.," and there are no clues within the message—or elsewhere in the forum—about Dan M.'s source of authority. Searching for "Dan M." at this Web site provided a list of the author's messages but offered no other information. The availability of Dan M.'s email address, however, made it easy to contact the author directly for verification. The following sentence shows how a text might refer to both the discussion forum message and what we learned through the subsequent email contact:

---

[2]Tina Kelley, "Whales in the Minnesota River?" *New York Times* 4 Mar. 1999, late ed.: G1+.

As we planned our route for hiking the Virgin River Narrows in Zion National Park, we followed the advice posted by "Dan M.," a self-described "semi-frequent" visitor to the park who had hiked the Narrows twice ("Dan M.," personal email).[3]

If you have no way to validate a Web author's legitimacy, do not rely on the information!

2 Publishing body

The *publishing body* for an Internet document is the **server** on which the file is stored, but there is no way for the server to guarantee the reliability of the information it stores. More important than the server's name are any names or logos appearing within the document that represent organizations that may stand behind the author's work. For example, you can be confident that Leslie Harris's essay "Writing Spaces: Using MOOs to Teach Composition and Literature," which appeared in *Kairos: A Journal for Teaching Writing in Webbed Environments* (Summer 1996), is valuable. *Kairos,* an electronic journal sponsored by the Alliance for Computers and Writing at <http://english.ttu.edu/kairos>, has an international reputation for publishing articles of high quality. However, if a site's sponsor is a commercial entity (i.e., the **domain name** ends in *.com*), consider whether material on the site is likely to be shaped by the sponsor's business goals.

Questions about a site's publisher don't always have obvious answers. For example, many print periodicals commonly considered authoritative sources of information (e.g., newspapers of record such as the *New York Times* and the *Los Angeles Times*) now sponsor Web sites ending with the *.com* **extension** . On the other hand, consider the well-known case of the Web sites <http://www.amnesty.org/tunisia> and <http://www.amnesty-tunisia.org>. The first is sponsored by the human rights group Amnesty International, the second by the Tunisian government. The sites present very different views of the human rights situation in that country—and yet their domain names could easily be confused.

---

[3]If this sentence were part of a documented essay, the list of works cited would include two entries for "Dan M."—one with the title "Re: Hiking the Narrows in Nov" and one for the personal email message.

3 Referral to and/or knowledge of other sources

Understanding the author's *"referral to and/or knowledge of other sources"* is probably the key to estimating the reliability of Internet source material. To find evidence that will help you make this judgment, you can use two approaches:

1. Examine the content of the document to see whether it represents other sources fairly.
2. Seek out other sources to see if the author has considered enough alternative views.

Of course, you may need guidance from others in the author's field in order to make an informed judgment. Here the Internet can play a key role by enabling you to search quickly for the names or ideas of others mentioned by the author. For example, you might subscribe to a **listserv** or participate in a **newsgroup** in the author's field, both to learn more about the context of the author's work and to be able to seek others' opinions if necessary.

4 Accuracy or verifiability

How you establish the *accuracy* of data you find on the Internet is not very different from how you establish the accuracy of print data, but the special features of **hypertext** often make your task easier. For example, an author quoting statistics from another Internet source will often include a direct link to the other source. Even though Internet sources that point to other documents in this fashion may not have traditional bibliographies, they are nonetheless well documented.

5 Currency

The *currency* of an Internet document refers to the history of its publication and any revisions. A document with no dating at all is less reliable (on this particular score) than one that lists numerous revisions; in the second case, the author shows greater respect for readers' information needs.

6 Checklists for evaluating sources

Another good source for evaluation techniques is "Evaluating Web Resources" from Widener University at <http://

www2.widener.edu/Wolfgram-Memorial-Library/web
evaluation/webeval.htm>. This document offers a step-
by-step approach to evaluating a Web site's authority,
accuracy, objectivity, currency, and coverage. Checklists
for five different categories of Web sites (business, reference, news, advocacy, and personal pages) provide
detailed questions to answer. Each checklist focuses on
verifying the legitimacy of the information and its sponsoring organization or individual(s). This highly struc-
tured approach differs from the more intuitive practice
described in 4d-1 through 4d-5, but the resulting evaluations of a Web site's reliability will be essentially the
same. Use whichever method you prefer!

7 Web site reviews

Many librarians and other professionals are publishing
extensive reviews of Web sites, focusing their comments
on the issues described here. The printed periodical
Choice, published by the American Library Association,
features about forty Web site reviews each month. You
can see sample reviews and obtain a two-month free
subscription at <http://www.choicereviews.org/rev170
choicescripts/>. For online reviews, consult the Internet
Reviews Archive maintained by *College and Research
Libraries News* at <http://www.bowdoin.edu/~samato
/IRA>. These collections are not likely to hold reviews
for all your Internet sources, but they do provide excellent examples of written evaluations, and they can help
you identify new sources in your subject area. The weekly *Chronicle of Higher Education* also publishes brief notes
about new Web sites in its "Internet Resources" section,
available online at <http://chronicle.com/free/resources>.
Use the *Chronicle* listings as pointers to sites that deserve
further attention.

4e Representing your evaluation in your writing

When you use an Internet source in your writing,
demonstrate your evaluation of the source's reliability
by carefully choosing a *signal verb* to show your understanding of the author's purpose (what the author is trying to achieve in his or her writing) and how successful
the author is in achieving that purpose. By using signal

verbs, you let readers know the context in which the source's statement should be viewed.

Consider the following quotation from a message that Jeremy Abrams posted in 1996 to the newsgroup <alt.philosophy.objectivism>:

> Science offers no substitute for the ethical concern of religion.

You can introduce your use of this quotation with a variety of signal verbs:

> Jeremy Abrams *says* that . . .
>
> Jeremy Abrams *believes* that . . .
>
> Jeremy Abrams *claims* that . . .
>
> Jeremy Abrams *argues* that . . .
>
> Jeremy Abrams *proves* that . . .

Your choice of the signal verb helps your reader understand both Abrams's intention and the degree to which he affirms and supports his statements. If you choose to use *proves* instead of *believes,* then you signal to your reader that the quotation in context proves by convincing evidence and persuasive logic that "science offers no substitute for the ethical concern of religion." If you choose the signal verb *say* instead of *prove,* you are reporting that Abrams makes his statement without any substantial support. Choose your signal verbs carefully so that they genuinely reflect the tone and substance of each cited source.

Box 4.2 lists some signal verbs you can use to show your readers how you have evaluated your sources. By using signal verbs to introduce and discuss Internet and print sources, you add integrity to your authorial voice and encourage your readers to trust the judgments you make in reporting and evaluating information.

Chapters 5 through 8 provide guidelines for citing and documenting Internet sources in four widely used styles. If you are required to follow a citation style not discussed here, and if that style doesn't cover Internet sources, you can adapt the style to fit the Internet sources you need to cite (using Appendix A as a guide) and then ask your instructor or editor to review your adaptation.

Box 4.2
Signal verbs for evaluating sources

acknowledges	develops	opposes
advises	diagnosis	organizes
agrees	disagrees	points to
allows	discusses	presents
analyzes	embraces	promotes
answers	emphasizes	proposes
appreciates	evaluates	recognizes
approves	examines	records
arranges	explains	regards
asserts	expresses	remarks
assumes	formulates	replies
believes	holds	reports
catalogs	illustrates	responds
charges	implies	reveals
claims	inspects	says
clarifies	interprets	states
classifies	introduces	suggests
considers	investigates	supports
creates	leaves us with	tells us
criticizes	lists	thinks
critiques	objects	wants to
declares	observes	wishes
describes	offers	wonders

Using MLA Style to Cite and Document Sources

This chapter's guidelines for citing **Internet** sources are based on the *MLA Handbook for Writers of Research Papers* (2003) by Joseph Gibaldi. The *MLA Handbook* advises that you acknowledge sources "by keying brief parenthetical citations in your text to an alphabetical list of works that appears at the end of the paper" (142). Widely used by writers in literature, language studies, and other fields in the humanities, the MLA style of documentation allows writers to keep texts "as readable and as free of disruptions as possible" (143).

The *MLA Handbook* provides information about the purposes of research; suggestions for choosing topics; recommendations for using libraries; guidance for composing outlines, drafts, notes, and bibliographies; and advice on spelling, punctuation, abbreviations, and other stylistic matters. It also presents a style for documenting sources and gives directions for citing print sources in the text and preparing a list of Works Cited. Thorough acquaintance with the *MLA Handbook* will, as its author promises, "help you become a writer whose work deserves serious consideration" (xv). This chapter follows the conventions of MLA citation style.

5a Using principles of MLA style to cite Internet sources

The *MLA Handbook* gives guidelines for making in-text references to print sources. The following section shows how you can apply the same principles to citing online sources in your text.

1 Link an in-text citation of an Internet source to a corresponding entry in the Works Cited.

According to the *MLA Handbook*, each text reference to an outside source must point clearly to a specific entry in the list of Works Cited. The essential elements of an in-text citation are the author's name (or the document's title, if no author is identified) and a page reference or other information showing where in a source cited material appears.

Create an in-text reference to an Internet source by using a signal phrase, a parenthetical citation, or both a previewing sentence and a parenthetical citation.

Box 5.1
Using italics and underlining in MLA style

The *MLA Handbook* provides the following advice for the use of italics and underlining in word-processed texts intended for print-only publication:

> Many word-processing programs and computer printers permit the reproduction of italic type. In material that will be graded, edited, or typeset, however, the type style of every letter and punctuation mark must be easily recognizable. Italic type is sometimes not distinctive enough for this purpose, and you can avoid ambiguity by using underlining when you intend italics. If you wish to use italics rather than underlining, check your instructor's or editor's preferences. (94)

However, when composing in **HTML,** don't substitute underlining for italics, because underlining in HTML indicates that the underlined text is an active **hypertext link.** (All HTML editing programs automatically underline any text linked to another hypertext or **Web site.**)

When composing Web documents, use italics for titles, for emphasis, and for words, letters, and numbers referred to as such. When you write with programs such as **email** that don't allow italics, type an underscore mark _like this_ before and after text you would otherwise italicize or underline.

Using a signal phrase   To introduce cited material consisting of a short quotation, paraphrase, or summary, use either a signal phrase set off by a comma or a signal verb with a *that* clause, as in the following examples. (See 4e for a discussion of signal phrases and verbs.)

> signal phrase

▶ According to Steven E. Landsburg, "if you know you're going to treasure something, you don't hesitate to buy it."

> signal phrase

▶ In his January 1991 letter to the editors of PMLA, Jason Mitchell suggests that the "pretentious gibberish" of modern literary critics--"Euro-jive," as he calls it--is often produced by English professors who need to prove that their professional status is equal to that of math and science faculty.

Here are the Works Cited entries for these two sources:

▶ Landsburg, Steven E. "Who Shall Inherit the Earth?" Slate 1 May 1997. 1 Oct. 1999 <http://www.slate.com/Economics/97-05-01/ Economics.asp>.

▶ Mitchell, Jason P. "PMLA Letter." Home page. 10 May 1997. 1 Nov. 1999 <http:// sunset.backbone.olemiss.edu/~jmitchel/ pmla.htm>.

Note that the Mitchell document's date of Internet publication is later than its original (1991) publication date.

Using a parenthetical citation   To identify the source of a quotation, paraphrase, or summary, place the author's last name in parentheses after the cited material.

▶ "Parents know in advance, and with near certainty, that they will be addicted to their children" (Landsburg).

▶ In response to Victor Brombert's 1990 MLA presidential address on the "politics of critical language," one correspondent suggests that "some literary scholars envy the scientists their wonderful jargon with its certainty and precision and thus wish to emulate it by creating formidably technical-sounding words of their own" (Mitchell).

Here are the Works Cited entries for these sources:

▶ Landsburg, Steven E. "Who Shall Inherit the Earth?" <u>Slate</u> 1 May 1997. 1 Oct. 1999 <http://www.slate.com/Economics/97-05-01/ Economics.asp>.

▶ Mitchell, Jason P. PMLA Letter. Home page. 10 May 1997. 1 Nov. 1999 <http:// sunset.backbone.olemiss.edu/~jmitchel/ pmla.htm>.

Using a previewing sentence and a parenthetical citation To introduce and identify the source of a long quotation (one comprising more than four lines in your essay or research paper), use a previewing sentence that ends in a colon. By briefly announcing the content of an extended quotation, a previewing sentence tells readers what to look for in the quotation. Indent the block quotation ten spaces (or two paragraph indents) from the left margin. At the end of the block quotation, cite the source in parentheses after the final punctuation mark.

▶ That the heroic and historically important deeds of previously unknown women should be included in history books is evident from the following notice:

> Event: April 26, 1777, Sybil Ludington. On the night of April 26, 1777, Sybil Ludington, age 16, rode through towns in New York and Connecticut to warn that the Redcoats were coming . . . to Danbury, CT. All very Paul Reverish, except Sybil completed HER ride, and SHE thus gathered enough volunteers to help beat back the British the next day. Her ride was twice the distance of Revere's. No poet immortalized (and faked) her accomplishments, but at least her hometown was renamed

after her. However, recently the National
Rifle Association established a Sybil Lud-
ington women's "freedom" award for merito-
rious service in furthering the purposes
of the NRA as well as use of firearms in
competition or in actual life-threatening
situations although Sybil never fired a
gun. (Stuber)

Here is the Works Cited entry:

▶ Stuber, Irene. "April 26, 1996: Episode 638."
<u>Women of Achievement and Herstory: A Fre-
quently-Appearing Newsletter</u>. 3 May 1996.
11 Dec. 1997 <http://www.imageworld.com/
vsp/istuber/woa/1996/woa638.asc>.

2 Substitute Internet text divisions for page numbers.

The examples in 5a-1 assume that an Internet source has
no internal divisions (pages, parts, chapters, headings,
sections, subsections). The *MLA Handbook*, however,
requires that you identify the location of any cited information as precisely as possible in parentheses. Because
Internet sources are rarely marked with page numbers,
you will not always be able to show exactly where cited
material comes from. If a source has internal divisions,
use these instead of page numbers in your citation. Be
sure to use divisions inherent in the document and not
those provided by your browsing software.

A text reference to a source with divisions may
appear in the text along with the author's name or be
placed in parentheses after a quotation, paraphrase, or
summary.

▶ As TyAnna Herrington notes in her Introduction,
"Nicholas Negroponte's <u>Being Digital</u> provides
another welcome not only into an age of technological ubiquity, but into a way of 'being'
with technology."

▶ "Negroponte's uncomplicated, personal tone fools
the reader into a sense that his theses are
simplistic" (Herrington "Introduction").

Here is the Works Cited entry:

▶ Herrington, TyAnna K. "Being Is Believing."
Rev. of <u>Being Digital</u>, by Nicholas Negroponte. <u>Kairos: A Journal for Teaching
Writing in Webbed Environments</u> 1.1 (1996).
24 May 1996 <http://english.ttu.edu/
kairos/1.1>. Path: Reviews.

3 Use source-reflective statements to show where cited material ends.

The MLA practice of parenthetical page-number citation
lets you indicate precisely where information from a
printed source ends. Many Internet sources, however,
appear as single screens, and MLA style does not require
parenthetical page citations for one-page works. By
analogy, a single-screen document cited in text needs no
page citation. To let your readers know where your use
of an Internet source with no text divisions ends, use a
source-reflective statement.

Source-reflective statements give you an opportunity
to assert your authorial voice. Writers use source-reflective statements to provide editorial comment, clarification, qualification, amplification, dissent, agreement,
and so on. In the following example, the absence of a
source-reflective statement creates uncertainty as to
where use of an Internet source ends.

▶ According to TyAnna Herrington, Nicholas Negroponte has the ability to make complex technological issues understandably simple. For those
who are not techno-philes, this is a blessing;
it allows them to apprehend the real significance of digital technology without feeling
that such ideas are too difficult to consider.

In the next example, the writer has added a source-reflective statement to show that use of the source has ended.

source-reflective statement

▶ According to TyAnna Herrington, Nicholas
Negroponte has the ability to make complex
technological issues understandably simple.
Herrington's observation is a good one.
It means that for those who are not techno-
philes, reading Negroponte is a blessing;
reading Negroponte allows one to apprehend the
real significance of digital technology without

```
feeling that such ideas are too difficult to
consider.
```

Here is the Works Cited entry:

▶ Herrington, TyAnna K. "Being Is Believing."
       Rev. of <u>Being Digital</u>, by Nicholas
       Negroponte. <u>Kairos: A Journal for
       Teaching Writing in Webbed Environments</u>
       1.1 (1996). 24 May 1996 <http://
       english.ttu.edu/kairos/1.1>. Path: Reviews.

For updates to MLA citation style, consult the MLA's
Web site <http://www.mla.org>.

5b Works Cited

When using MLA style, place a list of cited sources,
arranged alphabetically, after the text of your essay and
any explanatory notes. The *MLA Handbook* recommends
that you "draft the [Works Cited] section in advance, so
that you will know what information to give in parenthetical references as you write" (144). Doing this makes in-
text citation of sources easier by giving you an idea of what
in-text reference options will work best for each citation.

Referring to print sources, the *MLA Handbook* gives
the following general models for Works Cited entries:

Book

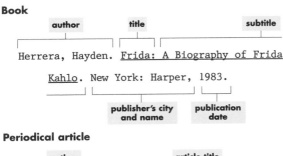

Periodical article

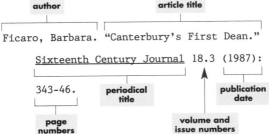

> **Box 5.2**
> **Using hypertext to document sources on the Web**
>
> The hypertext environment of the World Wide Web doesn't just alter the way you do research, it also lets you document sources in a new way—by using hypertext links. Electronic journals published on the Web are already replacing traditional notes, Works Cited listings, appendixes, and other supporting text with links to the documents being cited. To read more about hypertext documentation, see Chapter 9 in this book. For an example of how it works, see the sample paper for this chapter (described in 5c), or look at the format of Andrew Harnack and Eugene Kleppinger, "Beyond the *MLA Handbook*: Documenting Electronic Sources on the Internet" in *Kairos: A Journal for Teaching Writing in Webbed Environments* 1.2 (1996) at <http://english.ttu.edu/kairos/1.2 /inbox/mla.html> or any essay published in *Kairos* at <http://english.ttu.edu/kairos>.

The *MLA Handbook* also presents numerous variations that accommodate a variety of print sources (e.g., a multivolume work, an editorial). For detailed information on creating a Works Cited list, see Chapter 5 of the *MLA Handbook,* "Documentation: Preparing the List of Works Cited."

For writers creating in-text citations and Works Cited lists for online sources, the *MLA Handbook* provides the following general recommendations:

- Download or print any online material you plan to use, in case it becomes inaccessible online later.

- Don't introduce a hyphen at the break of a URL between two lines.

- If you must divide a URL between two lines, break it only *after* a slash (as we have done only in this chapter).[1]

Section 5.9 of the *MLA Handbook* includes models for numerous types of online sources (e.g., an online book, an advertisement, a multidisc publication). The following models for Works Cited entries, based on the recommendations of the *MLA Handbook,* cover the types of sources most often cited by student and professional writers.

---

[1]This instruction differs from the one in *Online!* (1d-2). We suggest that, for papers written in MLA style, you follow the MLA's recommendations.

1 World Wide Web site

When you document sources from the **World Wide Web**, the MLA suggests that your Works Cited entries contain as many items from the following list as are relevant and available:

- Name of the author, editor, compiler, translator, or site maintainer (if available and relevant), alphabetized by last name and followed by any appropriate abbreviations, such as *ed.*
- Title of a poem, short story, article, or other short work within a book, scholarly project, database, or periodical, in quotation marks
- Title of a book, in italics or underlined
- Name of the editor, compiler, or translator of a book (if applicable and if not cited earlier), preceded by any appropriate abbreviation, such as *Ed.*
- Publication information for any print version
- Title of a scholarly project, database, periodical, or professional or personal site (in italics or underlined), or, for a professional or personal site with no title, a description such as *home page*[2]
- Name of the editor of a scholarly project or database (if known)
- Version number (if not part of the title) or, for a journal, the volume, issue, or other identifying number
- Date of electronic publication or posting or latest update, whichever is most recent (if known)
- Name of any institution or organization sponsoring or associated with the Web site
- Date you accessed the source
- URL (in angle brackets)

Although no single entry will contain all these items of information, most Works Cited entries for Web sources will include the following basic information:

Online document

▶ Author's name (last name first). Document
    title. Date of Internet publication.
    Date of access <URL>.

---

[2]*Home page* is the spelling that MLA recommends.

Box 5.3
Formatting Works Cited entries in HTML

Some HTML editors don't let you easily indent the second line of a
Works Cited entry. In such instances, bullet the first line of an entry.

- Landsburg, Steven E. "Who Shall Inherit the
  Earth?" <u>Slate</u> 1 May 1997. 1 Oct. 1999 <http://www
  .slate.com/Economics/97-05-01/Economics.asp>.

- Mitchell, Jason P. "PMLA Letter." Home page. 10
  May 1997. 1 Nov. 1999 <http://sunset.backbone
  .olemiss.edu/~jmitchel/pmla.htm>.

To see how to document specific types of Web sources,
refer to the examples throughout this section.

Personal site

▶ Pellegrino, Joseph. Home page. 16 Dec. 1998.
     1 Oct. 1999 <http://www.english.eku.edu/
     pellegrino/personal.htm>.

Professional site

▶ <u>The William Faulkner Society Home Page</u>. Ed.
     Gail Mortimer. 16 Sept. 1999. 1 Oct. 1999
     <http://www.utep.edu/mortimer/faulkner/
     mainfaulkner.htm>.

▶ <u>NAIC Online</u>. 29 Sept. 1999. National Associa-
     tion of Investors Corporation. 1 Oct. 1999
     <http://www.better-investing.org>.

▶ <u>U. S. Department of Education (ED) Home Page</u>.
     29 Sept. 1999. US Dept. of Education. 1
     Oct. 1999 <http://www.ed.gov/index.html>.

▶ <u>William Faulkner on the Web</u>. 7 July 1999. U of
     Mississippi. 30 Sept. 1999 <http://
     www.mcsr.olemiss.edu/~egjbp/faulkner/
     faulkner.html>.

Book

An online book may be the electronic text of part or all
of a printed book, or a book-length document available
only on the Internet (e.g., a work of hyperfiction).

▶ Bird, Isabella L. <u>A Lady's Life in the Rocky
     Mountains</u>. New York, 1881. <u>Victorian Women
     Writers Project</u>. Ed. Perry Willett. 27 May
     1999. Indiana U. 4 Oct. 1999 <http://
     www.indiana.edu/~letrs/vwwp/bird/rocky.html>.

▶ Bryant, Peter J. "The Age of Mammals." <u>Bio-
        diversity and Conservation</u>. 28 Aug. 1999.
        4 Oct. 1999 <http://darwin.bio.uci.edu/
        ~sustain/bio65/lec02/b65lec02.htm>.

▶ Harnack, Andrew, and Eugene Kleppinger.
        Preface. <u>Online! A Reference Guide to
        Using Internet Sources</u>. Boston: Bedford/St.
        Martin's, 2000. 5 Jan. 2000 <http://
        www.bedfordstmartins.com/online>.

Article in an electronic journal (ejournal)

▶ Joyce, Michael. "On the Birthday of the
        Stranger (in Memory of John Hawkes)."
        <u>Evergreen Review</u> 102 (1999). 12 May 1999
        <http://www.evergreenreview.com/evexcite/
        joyce/index_ns.html>.

▶ Wysocki, Anne Frances. "Monitoring Order:
        Visual Desire, the Organization of Web
        Pages, and Teaching the Rules of Design."
        <u>Kairos: A Journal for Teachers of Writing
        in Webbed Environments</u> 3.2 (1998). 21 Oct.
        1999 <http://www.english.ttu.edu/kairos/
        3.2/features/wysocki/bridge.html>.

Article in an electronic magazine (ezine)

▶ Adler, Jerry. "Ghost of Everest." <u>Newsweek</u> 17 May
        1999. 19 May 1999 <http://newsweek.com/nwsrv/
        issue/20_99a/printed/us/so/so0120_1.htm>.

Newspaper article

▶ Wren, Christopher. "A Body on Mt. Everest, a
        Mystery Half-Solved." <u>New York Times on
        the Web</u> 5 May 1999. 13 May 1999 <http://
        search.nytimes.com/search/daily/bin/
        fastweb?getdoc+site+site+33726+0+wAAA+
        %22George%7EMallory%22>.

Review

▶ Parfit, Michael. Rev. of <u>The Climb: Tragic
        Ambitions on Everest</u>, by Anatoli Boukreev
        and G. Weston DeWalt. <u>New York Times on
        the Web</u> 7 Dec. 1997. 4 Oct. 1999 <http://
        search.nytimes.com/books/97/12/07/reviews/
        971207.07parfitt.html>.

Editorial

▶ "Public Should Try Revised Student Achievement
Test." Editorial. <u>Lexington Herald-Leader</u>
13 Apr. 1999. 4 Oct. 1999 <http://
www.kentuckyconnect.com/heraldleader/news/
041399/editorialdocs/413test-1.htm>.

Letter to the editor

▶ Gray, Jeremy. Letter. <u>Lexington Herald-Leader</u>.
7 May 1999. 7 May 1999 <http://
www.kentuckyconnect.com/heraldleader/news/
050799/lettersdocs/507letters.htm>.

Government publication

▶ United States. Senate Committee on the Judiciary.
<u>Children, Violence, and the Media: A Report
for Parents and Policy Makers</u>. By Orrin
G. Hatch. 14 Sept. 1999. 18 Feb. 2003
<http://judiciary.senate.gov/oldsite/
mediavio.htm>.

Scholarly project or information database

▶ <u>Center for Reformation and Renaissance Studies</u>.
Ed. Laura E. Hunt and William Barek. May
1998. U of Toronto. 11 May 1999 <http://
CITD.SCAR.UTORONTO.CA/crrs/index.html>.

▶ <u>The Internet Movie Database</u>. May 1999. Internet
Movie Database Ltd. 11 May 1999 <http://
us.imdb.com>.

Short text within a larger project or database

▶ Whitman, Walt. "Beat! Beat! Drums!" <u>Project
Bartleby Archive</u>. Ed. Steven van Leeuwen.
May 1998. Columbia U. 11 May 1999
<http://www.columbia.edu/acis/bartleby/
whitman/whit224.html>.

Other Web sources

When documenting other Web sources—for example, an
audio or film clip, a map, or a painting—provide a
descriptive phrase (e.g., *map*) if needed.

▶ di Bondone, Giotto. <u>The Mourning of Christ</u>.
1305. WebMuseum, Paris. 1 June 1999

<http://www.ibiblio.org/wm/paint/auth/
giotto/mourning-christ/mourning-christ.jpg>.

▶ "Methuen, Massachusetts." Map. <u>U.S. Gazeteer</u>.
     US Census Bureau. 4 Oct. 1999 <http://
     www.census.gov/cgi-bin/gazetteer>.

2 Material from a subscription service

To document an article or other material accessed
through a library or institutional subscription service
such as EBSCOhost or Lexis-Nexis, provide the following information:

- Publication information for the source
- Name of the database, in italics or underlined
- Name of the service
- Name of the library
- Date of access
- URL of the subscription service's homepage, if
  known

▶ Maynard, W. Barksdale. "Thoreau's House at
     Walden." <u>Art Bulletin</u> 81 (1999): 303-25.
     <u>Academic Search Premier</u>. EBSCOhost.
     Eastern Kentucky U Lib., Richmond.   19
     Nov. 2002 <http://www.ebscohost.com>.

3 Email message

To document an email message, provide the following
information:

- Author's name
- Subject line, in quotation marks
- Description of message that includes recipient (e.g.,
  e-mail to the author)[3]
- Date of sending

▶ Kleppinger, Eugene. "How to Cite Information
     from the Web." E-mail to Andrew Harnack.
     10 Jan. 1999.

---

[3]*E-mail* is the spelling that the MLA recommends.

4 Web discussion forum posting

To document a posting to a **Web discussion forum**, provide the following information:

- Author's name
- Title of posting, in quotation marks
- Phrase *online posting*
- Date of posting
- Name of forum
- Date of access
- URL, in angle brackets

▶ Colleen. "Climbing Questions." Online posting. 20 Mar. 1999. Climbing Forum. 27 May 1999 <http://www2.gorp.com/forums/ Index.cfm?CFApp=55&Message_ID=18596>.

▶ Marcy, Bob. "Think They'll Find Any Evidence of Mallory & Irvine?" Online posting. 30 Apr. 1999. Mt. Everest >99 Forum. 28 May 1999 <http://everest.mountainzone.com/99/forum>.

5 Listserv message

To document a **listserv** message, provide the following information:

- Author's name
- Subject line, in quotation marks
- Phrase *online posting*
- Date of posting
- Name of listserv
- Date of access
- Address of listserv, in angle brackets

▶ Holland, Norman. "Re: Colorless Green Ideas." Online posting. 30 May 1999. Psyart. 1 June 1999 <http://web.clas.ufl.edu/ipsa/ psyart.htm>.

▶ Parente, Victor. "On Expectations of Class Participation." Online posting. 27 May 1996. Philosed. 29 May 1996 <philosed@sued.syr.edu>.

6 Newsgroup message

To document information posted in a **newsgroup** discussion, provide the following information:

- Author's name
- Subject line, in quotation marks
- Phrase *online posting*
- Date of posting
- Date of access
- Name of newsgroup with prefix *news:*, in angle brackets

▶ Kaipiainen, Petri. "Re: Did Everest see Everest?" Online posting. 4 May 1999. 2 June 1999 <news:rec.climbing>.

If, after following all the suggestions in 4c-3, you cannot determine the author's name, then use the author's email address, enclosed in angle brackets, as the main entry. When deciding where in your Works Cited to insert such a source, treat the first letter of the email address as though it were capitalized.

▶ <lrm583@aol.com>. "Thinking of Adoption." 26 May 1996. 29 May 1996 <news:alt.adoption>.

7 Real-time communication

To document a **real-time communication**, such as those posted in **MUDs**, **MOOs**, and **IRCs**, provide the following information:

- Name of speaker(s) (if known)
- Description of event
- Date of event
- Forum (e.g., Diversity University)
- Date of access
- URL or other Internet address, in angle brackets

▶ Fox, Rita. "ENG 301 Class MOO: Concept mapping for Web project." 2 Feb. 1999. Diversity University. 3 Feb. 1999 <http://moo.duets.org:8888>.

▶ Sowers, Henry, Miram Fields, and Jane Gurney.
     "Online collaborative conference." 29 May
     1999. LinguaMOO. 29 May 1999 <telnet://
     lingua.utdallas.edu:8888>.

8 Telnet, FTP, and gopher sites

Telnet site

The most common use of **telnet** is for participation in **real-time communication** (see 5b-6). Although the use of telnet for document retrieval has declined dramatically with increased Web access to texts, numerous archived documents are available only by telnet. To document a telnet site or a file available via telnet, provide the following information:

* Name of author or agency
* Title of document
* Date of publication
* Date of access
* Telnet address, in angle brackets
* Directions for accessing document

▶ Environmental Protection Agency. "About the
     Clean Air Act (CAA) Database." 2 June
     1999 <telnet://fedworld.gov>. Path:
     Regulatory Agencies.

FTP site

To document a file available for downloading via **file transfer protocol**, provide the following information:

* Name of author or file
* Title of document
* Size of document (if relevant), in brackets
* Any print publication information, italicized or underlined where appropriate
* Date of online publication, if available
* Date of access
* Complete FTP address, in angle brackets

▶ "everest2.gif" [535K]. 4 Apr. 1993. 3 June
     1999 <ftp://ftp.ntua.gr/pub/images/views/
     sorted.by.type/Mountains/everest2.gif>.

▶ Mathews, J. Preface. <u>Numerical Methods for
  Mathematics, Science, and Engineering</u>. 2nd
  ed. N.p.: Prentice Hall, 1992. 8 June 1999
  <ftp://ftp.ntua.gr/pub/netlib/textbook/
  index.html>.

Gopher site

The **gopher** search protocol brings text files from all over the world to your computer. Popular in the early 1990s, especially at universities, gopher was a step toward the **World Wide Web**'s **hypertext transfer protocol (HTTP)**. Although the advent of **HTML** documents and their retrieval on the Web has diminished the use of gopher, many documents can still be accessed through Web browsers.

To document material obtained by using gopher, provide the following information:

- Author's name
- Title of document
- Any print publication information, italicized or underlined where appropriate
- Date of online publication
- Date of access
- Gopher address, in angle brackets
- Directions for accessing document

▶ Goody, Jack. "History and Anthropology:
  Convergence and Divergence." <u>Bulletin
  of the Institute of Ethnology</u>, 75.2 (1993).
  2 June 1999 <gopher://gopher.sinica.edu.tw/
  00/ioe/engbull/75b.txt>. Path: Anthropology.

5c   Sample MLA-style hypertext essay

The *Online!* Web site (http://www.bedfordstmartins.com/online) features a sample MLA style Web essay. Figures 5.1–5.3 show, respectively, the contents page, a sample text page, and part of the Works Cited page of that essay. For more detailed advice on how to compose a hypertext essay, see 9d.

Work Cited

Gibaldi, Joseph. *MLA Handbook for Writers of Research Papers.* New York: Mod. Lang. Assn., 2003.

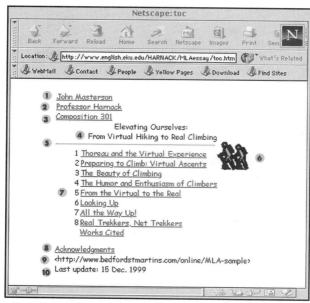

Figure 5.1
Title page of MLA-style hypertext essay

1. Author's name with *mailto:* link

2. Instructor's name with link to instructor's homepage

3. Course name and section number with link to course information

4. Title and subtitle

5. Optional use of horizontal line to separate table of contents from title

6. Optional use of fast-loading image or graphic repeated on subsequent pages to link pages visually

7. Table of contents with each entry linked to relevant page of essay

8. Link to optional acknowledgments page

9. URL

10. Notice of last update

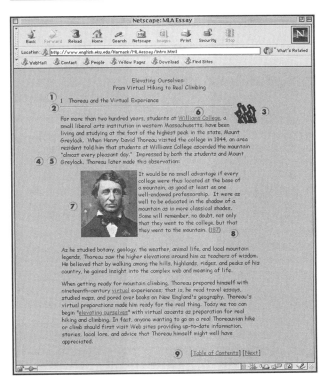

Figure 5.2
Sample page from body of MLA-style hypertext essay

1. Header corresponding to page's title in table of contents

2. Optional use of horizontal rule to separate header from text

3. Optional use of image or graphic

4. Single-spaced text paragraphs of readable length

5. Ample white space around paragraphs and illustrations

6. Hypertext links where appropriate

7. Use of quick-loading images, tables, and/or figures to complement text

8. Links to content notes and Works Cited

9. Navigation links to table of contents and previous and next pages

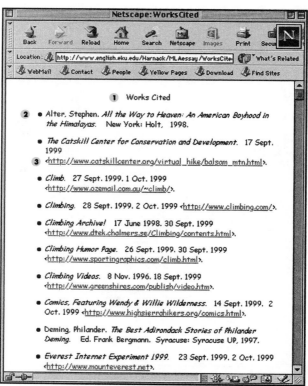

Figure 5.3
Works Cited page of MLA-style hypertext essay

1 Title

2 Entries formatted as bulleted list

3 Links to URLs of all online sources

CHAPTER SIX

Using APA Style to Cite and Document Sources

The fifth edition of the *Publication Manual of the American Psychological Association* (2001) provides documentation advice for writers in the social sciences. Written primarily for authors preparing manuscripts for professional publication in scholarly journals, the manual discusses manuscript content and organization, writing style, and manuscript preparation. It also offers advice for student writers in an appendix.

The *Publication Manual* instructs writers to document quotations, paraphrases, summaries, and other information from sources as follows: "Document your study throughout the text by citing by author and date the works you used in your research. This style of citation briefly identifies the source for readers and enables them to locate the source of information in the alphabetical reference list at the end of the article" (p. 207). When using APA style, consult the *Publication Manual* for general style requirements (e.g., style for metric units) and for advice on preparing manuscripts and electronic texts. This chapter follows the conventions of APA citation style.

6a Using principles of APA style to cite internet sources

The *Publication Manual* gives guidelines for making in-test references to print sources. The following section shows how you can apply the same principles to citing online sources in your text.[1]

1 Link an in-text citation of an Internet source to a corresponding entry in the References.

In APA style, each text reference is linked to a specific entry in the list of References. The essential elements of an in-text citation are the author's last name (or the document's title, if no author is identified) and the date of publication. Information such as a page or chapter number may be added to show where in a source cited material appears.

Create an in-text reference to an Internet source by using a signal phrase, a parenthetical citation, or both a previewing sentence and a parenthetical citation.

**Box 6.1
Using italics and underlining in APA style**

APA style recommends the use of italics, rather than underlining, for certain elements (e.g., book and journal titles). Use underlining only if your instructor requires it or if your word-processing program can't produce italics. However, the use of underlining to represent italics becomes a problem when you compose texts for online publication. On the World Wide Web, underlining in a document indicates that the underlined word or phrase is an active hypertext link. (All HTML editing programs automatically underline any text linked to another hypertext or Web site.)

When composing Web documents, avoid underlining. Instead, use italics for titles, for emphasis, and for words, letters, and numbers referred to as such. When you write with programs such as email that don't allow italics, type an underscore mark _like this_ before and after text you would otherwise italicize or underline.

---

[1]For final print copy, the *Publication Manual* specifies the "hanging indent" format for references, with each entry's first line set flush left and subsequent lines indented. Unless your instructor suggests otherwise, it is the format we recommend. Note, however, that APA permits the use of the reverse style (first lines indented, subsequent lines set flush left) in a manuscript if the writer's word-processing program cannot produce a hanging indent.

Using a signal phrase   To introduce a short quotation, paraphrase, or summary, mention the author's name either in an introductory signal phrase or in a parenthetical reference immediately following the signal phrase and containing the publication date. (See 4e for a discussion of signal phrases and verbs.)

> signal phrase

▶ Benton Foundation (1998) reported that "families who lack phone service have trouble contacting utilities and social service agencies to seek benefits for which they are qualified" (chap. 2, "Societal Priorities").

> signal phrase

▶ According to one study (Benton Foundation, 1998), low-income communities are less aggressive about demanding services from communications providers because members tend not to see much value in new technologies (chap. 2, "Lack of Political Clout").

Here is the References entry for this source:

▶ Benton Foundation (1998). <u>Losing ground bit by bit: Low-income communities in the information age</u> [Electronic version]. Retrieved June 27, 2001, from http://www.benton.org /Library/Low-Income/two.html

Using a parenthetical citation after cited material   Place the author's name and the source's date of publication in parentheses immediately after the end of the cited material.

▶ Families with no telephone service have difficulty accessing social services for which they are qualified (Benton Foundation, 1998, chap. 2, "Societal Priorities").

Using a previewing sentence and a parenthetical citation   To introduce and identify the source of a long quotation (one comprising 40 or more words), use a previewing sentence that names the author and ends in a colon. By briefly announcing the content of an extended quotation, a previewing sentence tells readers what to look for in the quotation. Indent the block quotation five spaces (or one paragraph indent). At the end of the quotation, after the final punctuation mark, indicate in parentheses any text division that indicates the quotation's location in the source document.

H. R. Varian (1997, June 11) suggested one way a professional organization might develop and publish an electronic journal:

> First, the journal assembles a board of editors. The function of the board is not only to provide a list of luminaries to grace the front cover of the journal; they will actually have to do some work.
>
> Authors submit (electronic) papers to the journal. These papers have 3 parts: a one-paragraph abstract, a 5-page summary, and a 20- to 30-page conventional paper. The abstract is a standard part of academic papers and needs no further discussion. The summary is modeled after the *Papers and Proceedings Issue of the American Economic Review*: it should describe what question the author addresses, what methods were used to answer the question, and what the author found. The summary should be aimed at as broad an audience as possible. This summary would then be linked to the supporting evidence: mathematical proofs, econometric analysis, data sets, simulations, etc. The supporting evidence could be quite technical, and would probably end up being similar to current published papers in structure. (section 7.2)

Here is the References entry:

▶ Varian, H. R. (1997, June 11). <u>The future of electronic journals.</u> Paper presented at the 1997 Scholarly Communication and Technology Conference. Retrieved June 27, 2001, from http://arl.cni.org/scomm/scat/varian.html

2 Substitute Internet text divisions for page numbers.

The *Publication Manual* (2001) requires that, in citing a print source, "[you] give the author, year, and page number in parentheses" (p. 120). Because Internet sources are rarely marked with page numbers, you will not always be able to show exactly where cited material comes from. If a source has numbered internal divisions (such as sections or paragraphs), use these instead of page numbers in your citation, making use of the ¶ symbol or the abbreviations *chap.* and *para.* Be sure to use divisions inherent in the document and not those provided by your browsing software.

▶ J. McGann (1995) pointed out that even decentered hypertexts are nevertheless always ordered: "To say that a HyperText is not centrally organized does not mean--at least does not mean to me--that the HyperText structure has no governing order(s), even at a theoretical level" ("Coda: A Note on the Decentered Text").

Here is the References entry:

▶ McGann, J. (1995). <u>The rationale of HyperText.</u>
    Retrieved June 27, 2001, from University
    of Virginia, Institute for Advanced
    Technology in the Humanities Web site:
    http://jefferson.village.virginia.edu
    /public/jjm2f/rationale.html

3 Use source-reflective statements to show where cited material ends.

Many Internet sources appear as single screens. To let your readers know where your use of a single-screen Internet source with no text divisions ends, use a *source-reflective statement.*

Source-reflective statements give you an opportunity to assert your authorial voice. Writers use source-reflective statements to provide editorial comment, clarification, qualification, amplification, dissent, agreement, and so on. In the following example, the absence of a source-reflective statement creates uncertainty as to whether the writer has finished citing an Internet source or has merely moved from quoting directly to paraphrasing.

▶ Sosteric (1996, Introduction) has noted that "exponential growth of the primary literature coupled with an explosive growth in the cost of distributing scholarly information has put serious strain on the financial resources of libraries and universities." This demand for and cost of distributing primary literature

> suggests that we can expect more electronic
> journals to appear online in the next few years
> --surely a benefit to scholarly communication.

In the next example, the writer has added a source-reflective statement to show that use of the source has ended.

▶ Sosteric (1996, Introduction) has noted that
  "exponential growth of the primary literature
  coupled with an explosive growth in the cost
  of distributing scholarly information has put
  serious strain on the financial resources of
  libraries and universities." Sosteric's observation suggests that the demand for and cost
  of distributing primary literature means we
  can expect more electronic journals to appear
  online in the next few years--surely a benefit
  to scholarly communication.

> **source-reflective statement**

Here is the References entry:

▶ Sosteric, M. (1996). Electronic journals:
      The grand information future? <u>Electronic
      Journal of Sociology,</u> 4(1). Retrieved June
      27, 2001, from http://www.sociology.org
      /content/vol002.002/sosteric.html

6b References

When using APA style, place a list of cited sources, arranged alphabetically, after the text of your essay but before any appendixes or explanatory notes. The *Publication Manual* (2001) gives the following general models for References entries:

Book

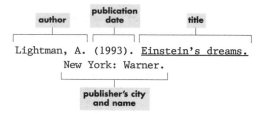

Lightman, A. (1993). <u>Einstein's dreams.</u>
      New York: Warner.

Periodical article

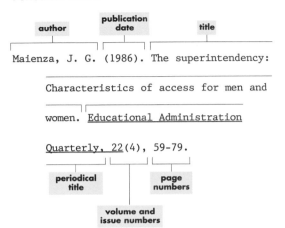

Maienza, J. G. (1986). The superintendency:

Characteristics of access for men and

women. Educational Administration

Quarterly, 22(4), 59-79.

The *Publication Manual* also presents numerous variations that accommodate a variety of print sources (e.g., translations, government documents). For detailed information on creating a References list, see Chapter 3 of the *Publication Manual,* "APA Editorial Style."

Extending the citation practice of the *Publication Manual* to include Internet sources produces the following generic model:

Online document

▶ Author's name (last name, first and any middle initials). (Date of Internet publication). Document title. Title of complete work [if applicable]. Retrieval statement.

Internet sources differ in the kinds of information that are important for retrieval, and the model for each type of source reflects the information needed to retrieve that source. The following models enable you to document Internet sources in a manner consistent with the principles of APA style.

1 World Wide Web site

The *Publication Manual* notes that "the vast majority of Internet sources cited in APA journals are those accessed via the Web" (p. 269). It instructs authors using and citing Web sources to observe the following guidelines:

Box 6.2
Using hypertext to document sources on the Web

The hypertext environment of the World Wide Web doesn't just alter the way you do research, it also lets you document sources in a new way—by using hypertext links. Electronic journals published on the Web are already replacing traditional notes, References listings, appendixes, and other supporting text with links to the documents being cited. To read more about hypertext documentation, see Chapter 9 in this book. For an example of how it works, see the sample paper for this chapter (described in 6c), or look at articles published in the *Electronic Journal of Sociology* at <http://www.sociology.org>.

- Where possible and relevant, provide URL references to specific documents rather than home or menu pages.
- Provide URLs that work.

If your paper will be available online as an updatable hypertext essay, make a point of testing the URLs in your references regularly. Consider replacing (with a reference to a later version) or simply dropping any sources whose original URLs no longer work.

To cite an entire Web site (but not a specific document on the site), simply give the site's URL in the text:

▶ Rainbow MOO is a virtual space designed especially for teachers and their elementary-school students (http://it.uwp.edu/rainbow).

To document a specific file, provide as much as possible of the following information:

- Author's name (if available)
- Date of publication or update or date of retrieval, in parentheses
- Title or description of document
- Title of complete work (if relevant), in italics or underlined
- Other relevant information (volume number, page numbers, etc.)
- Retrieval date statement
- URL

For more specific guidance, see the various sample citations in this section.

Book

An online book may be the electronic text of part or all of a printed book, or a book-length document available only on the Internet.

▶ Bryant, P. (1999). <u>Biodiversity and Conserva-
    tion.</u> Retrieved October 4, 1999, from
    http://darwin.bio.uci.edu/~sustain/bio65
    /Titlpage.htm

Article in an electronic journal (ejournal)

▶ Fine, M., & Kurdek, L. A. (1993). Reflections
    on determining authorship credit and
    authorship order on faculty-student
    collaborations. <u>American Psychologist, 48,</u>
    1141-1147. Retrieved June 7, 1999, from
    http://www.apa.org/journals/amp/kurdek.html

Abstract

▶ Isaac, J. D., Sansone, C., & Smith, J. L.
    (1999, May). Other people as a source of
    interest in an activity. <u>Journal of Exper-
    imental Social Psychology, 35,</u> 239-265.
    Abstract retrieved June 7, 1999, from
    IDEAL database Website: http://www.europe
    .idealibrary.com

Article in an electronic magazine (ezine)

▶ Adler, J. (1999, May 17). Ghost of Everest.
    <u>Newsweek.</u> Retrieved May 19, 1999, from
    http://newsweek.com/nwsrv/issue/20_99a
    /printed/us/so/so0120_1.htm

Box 6.3
Breaking URLs in APA style

The *Publication Manual* (p. 271) gives the following options for breaking URLs:

- After a slash
- Before a period

These instructions differ slightly from the ones in 1d-2 of this book. We suggest that, for papers written in APA style, you follow the APA's recommendations.

Newspaper article

▶ Azar, B., & Martin, S. (1999, October). APA's
      Council of Representatives endorses new
      standards for testing, high school psy-
      chology. <u>APA Monitor.</u> Retrieved October
      7, 1999, from http://www.apa.org/monitor
      /in1.html

Review

▶ Parfit, M. (1997, December 7). Breathless.
      [Review of the book <u>The climb: Tragic
      ambitions on Everest</u>]. <u>New York Times on
      the Web.</u> Retrieved October 7, 1999, from
      the World Wide Web: http://search.nytimes
      .com/books/97/12/07/reviews/971207
      .07parfitt.html

Letter to the editor

▶ Gray, J. (1999, May 7). Pesticides linger in
      land and air—and in our bodies [Letter to
      the editor]. <u>Lexington Herald-Leader.</u>
      Retrieved October 7, 1999, from http://www
      .kentuckyconnect.com/heraldleader/news
      /050799/lettersdocs/507letters.htm

Government publication

▶ Bush, G. (1989, April 12). Principles of ethi-
      cal conduct for government officers and
      employees. Exec. Order No. 12674. Pt. 1.
      Retrieved November 18, 1997, from http://
      www.usoge.gov/exorders/eo12674.html

2 Material from a subscription service

To document an article or other material accessed
through a library or institutional subscription service
such as EBSCOhost or Lexis-Nexis, provide

• Publication information for the source

• Retrieval statement, including the name of the specific database used (do not include the URL or name
  of the subscription service)

▶ Kowalski, R. M. (2002). Whining, griping, and
      complaining: Positivity in the negativity.
      <u>Journal of Clinical Psychology, 58,</u>

1023-1035. Retrieved November 7, 2002,
from Academic Search Premier database.

3 Email message

The *Publication Manual* (p. 214) recommends that email[3]
messages from individuals be cited as personal communications, and therefore not be included in the References. Here is how an in-text parenthetical reference to a
personal email message might look:

▶ Bryan Burgin (personal communication, November
18, 1998) notified me that my proposal had been
accepted.

In general, the APA discourages the inclusion in the
References of communications that are not archived
anywhere and therefore cannot be retrieved for verification. The *Publication Manual* (p. 214) cautions that
"computer networks (including the Internet) currently
provide a casual forum for communicating, and what
you cite should have scholarly relevance."

Always evaluate the validity of your source, particularly if you do not personally know the author of an
email message. (See 4c-3 and 4d.)

4 Web discussion forum posting

To document a posting to a **Web discussion forum**, provide the following information:

• Author's name
• Date of posting, in parentheses
• Title of posting
• Posting statement

▶ Abeles, T. (1999, May 21). Technology and the
future of higher education. Formal discussion initiation. Message posted to http://
ifets.gmd.de/discussions/discuss_apr99.html

▶ Marcy, B. (1999, April 3). Think they'll find
any evidence of Mallory & Irvine? Message
posted to http://everest.mountainzone.com
/99/forum

---

[3]Note that the APA's preferred spelling is *e-mail*.

5 Listserv message

To document a **listserv** message, provide the following information:

- Author's name
- Date of posting, in parentheses
- Subject line of posting
- Posting and archival statement

▶ Robertson, David M. (2001, June 24). Re: Lebanese cuisine books (1961, 1966) [June 2001, week 4, Msg 18.2]. Message posted to the American Dialect Society's ADS-L electronic mailing list, archived at http://listserv.linguistlist.org/archives/ads-l.html

Note that the *Publication Manual* recommends that the term *electronic mailing list* be used instead of *listserv.*

6 Newsgroup message

To document information posted in a **newsgroup** discussion, provide the following information:

- Author's name (or screen name, if real name is unknown)
- Date of posting, in parentheses
- Subject line
- Posting statement

▶ Brett. (1999, June 6). Experiments proving the collective unconscious. Message posted to news://alt.psychology.jung

7 Real-time communication

To document a **real-time communication**, such as those posted in **MOOs**, **MUDs**, and **IRCs**, provide the following information:

- Name of speaker(s) (if known), or name of site
- Date of event, in parentheses
- Title of event (if relevant)

- Type of communication (e.g., group discussion, personal interview), if not indicated elsewhere in entry
- Retrieval statement

▶ Fox, R. (1999, February 2). ENG 301 Class MOO:
    Concept mapping for Web project. Retrieved
    February 3, 1999, from http://moo.du.org
    :8000

▶ Sowers, H., Fields, M., & Gurney, J. (1999,
    29 May). Online collaborative conference.
    Retrieved 29 May, 1999, from LinguaMOO:
    telnet://lingua.utdallas.edu:8888

8 Telnet, FTP, and gopher sites

Telnet site

The most common use of **telnet** is for participation in
real-time communication (see 6b-6). Although the use
of telnet for document retrieval has declined dramatically with increased Web access to texts, numerous
archived documents are available only by telnet. To document a telnet site or a file available via telnet, provide
the following information:

- Name of author or agency
- Date of publication, in parentheses
- Title of document
- Retrieval statement, including name of database
- Telnet address with directions for accessing document

▶ Environmental Protection Agency. (1990).
    About the Clean Air Act (CAA) database.
    Retrieved June 2, 1999, from FedWorld
    Information Network: telnet fedworld.gov
    go Regulatory Agencies

FTP site

To document a file available for downloading via **file
transfer protocol**, provide the following information:

- Name of author or file
- Date of publication, in parentheses
- Size of document (if relevant)

- Title of document
- Retrieval statement
- Complete FTP address

▶ everest2.gif. (1993, April 4). 535K. Image of
    Mt. Everest. Retrieved June 3, 1999, from
    ftp://ftp.ntua.gr/pub/images/views/sorted
    .by.type/Mountains/everest2.gif

▶ Mathews, J. (1992). Preface. In <u>Numerical methods
    for mathematics, science, and engineering.</u>
    Retrieved June 8, 1999, from ftp://ftp.ntua
    .gr/pub/netlib/textbook/index.html

Gopher site

The **gopher** search protocol brings text files from all over the world to your computer. Popular during the early 1990s, especially at universities, gopher was a step toward the **World Wide Web**'s **hypertext transfer protocol (HTTP)**. Although the advent of **HTML** documents and their retrieval on the Web has diminished the use of gopher, many documents can still be accessed.

To document material obtained by using gopher, provide the following information:

- Author's name
- Date of online publication, in parentheses
- Title of document
- Any print publication information, italicized or underlined where appropriate
- Retrieval statement
- Gopher address with directions for accessing document

▶ Goody, J. (1993, Spring). History and anthro-
    pology: Convergence and divergence.
    <u>Bulletin of the Institute of Ethnology,</u>
    <u>75</u> (2). Academia Sinica, 75. Retrieved
    June 2, 1999, from gopher://gopher.sinica
    .edu.tw/00/ioe/engbull/75b.txt

6c Sample APA-style hypertext essay

The *Online!* Web site (http://www.bedfordstmartins .com/online) features a sample APA-style Web essay.

Figures 6.1–6.4 show, respectively, the contents page, the abstract page, a sample text page, and part of the References page of that essay. For more detailed advice on how to compose a hypertext essay, see 9d.

Reference

American Psychological Association. (2001). *Publication Manual of the American Psychological Association* (5th ed.). Washington, DC: American Psychological Association.

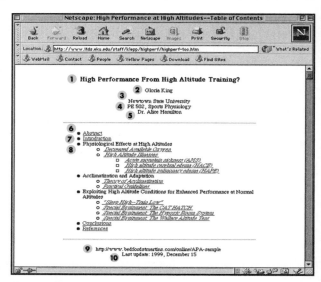

Figure 6.1
Title page of APA-style hypertext essay

1 Title

2 Author's name

3 Institution's name

4 Course name and section number

5 Instructor's name

6 Optional use of horizontal line to separate table of contents from title

7 Table of contents with each entry linked to relevant page of essay

8 Link to abstract

9 URL

10 Notice of last update

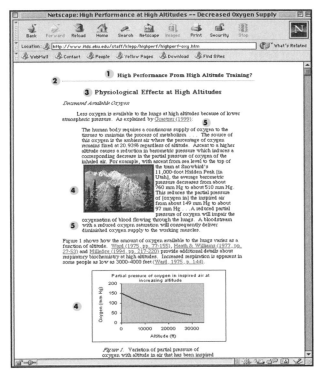

Figure 6.2
Sample page from body of APA-style hypertext essay

1 Running head

2 Optional use of horizontal rule to separate running head from text

3 Header corresponding to page's title in table of contents

4 Use of quick-loading images, tables, and/or figures to complement text

5 Links to References

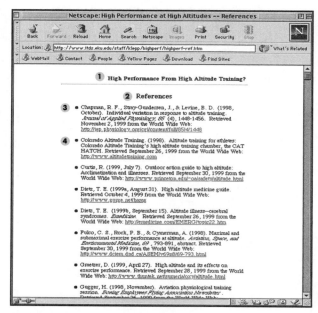

Figure 6.3
References page of APA-style hypertext essay

❶ Running head

❷ Title

❸ Entries formatted as bulleted list

❹ Links to URLs of all online sources

CHAPTER SEVEN

Using *Chicago* Style to Cite and Document Sources

This chapter's guidelines for citing **Internet** sources are based on the principles presented in the fourteenth edition of *The Chicago Manual of Style*.[1] The *Chicago Manual* offers two documentation styles, one using notes and bibliographies, the other using author-date citations and lists of references. The *Chicago Manual* also gives guidelines for spelling and punctuation and discusses the treatment of numbers, quotations, illustrations, tables, foreign languages, mathematical symbols, abbreviations, and so on.

To mark citations in the text, the *Chicago Manual*'s note-bibliography style places a superscript number after each quotation, paraphrase, or summary. Citations are numbered sequentially throughout the text, and each citation corresponds to a numbered note containing publication information about the source cited. Such notes are called *footnotes* when printed at the foot of a page and *endnotes* when printed at the end of an essay, chapter, or book. These notes generally serve two purposes: to cite

---

[1]*The Chicago Manual of Style,* 14th ed. (Chicago: University of Chicago Press, 1993). When this chapter cites the *Chicago Manual,* it does so in footnotes such as this one.

sources and to make cross-references to previous notes. This chapter follows the conventions of the *Chicago Manual*'s note-bibliography style.

7a Adapting *Chicago* style to cite Internet sources

Although the *Chicago Manual* provides some advice for documenting information from computerized data services, computer programs, and electronic documents, it contains no advice on documenting Internet sources. The following recommendations adapt the *Chicago Manual*'s guidelines and models to Internet sources.

1 Introduce the source of a short quotation, paraphrase, or summary by using either a signal phrase set off by a comma or a signal verb with a *that* clause.

The following two examples show how signal phrases can be used to introduce cited material. (See 4e for a discussion of signal phrases and verbs.)

signal phrase

▶ According to Brendan P. Kehoe, "We are truly in an information society. Now more than ever, moving vast amounts of information quickly across great distances is one of our most pressing needs."

signal phrase

▶ Brendan P. Kehoe reminds us that "we are truly in an information society. Now more than ever, moving vast amounts of information quickly across great distances is one of our most pressing needs."[1]

Here is the note for this source:

▶   1. Brendan P. Kehoe, <u>Zen and the Art of the Internet,</u> January 1992, <http://freenet.buffalo .edu/~popmusic/zen10.txt> (4 June 1999), Network Basics.

Box 7.1
Using italics and underlining in *Chicago* style

Chicago style recommends italicizing certain elements (e.g., book and journal titles) in printed text. Use underlining if your instructor requires it or if your typewriter or word-processing program can't produce italics. However, the use of underlining to represent italics becomes a problem when you compose texts for online publication. On the World Wide Web, underlining in a document indicates that the underlined word or phrase is an active hypertext link. (All HTML editing programs automatically underline any text linked to another hypertext or Web site.)

When composing Web documents, avoid underlining. Instead, use italics for titles, for emphasis, and for words, letters, and numbers referred to as such. When you write with programs such as email that don't allow italics, type an underscore mark _like this_ before and after text you would otherwise italicize or underline.

2 **Link an in-text citation of an Internet source to a corresponding note.**

According to *Chicago* style, the first note for a given source should include all the information necessary to identify and locate the source: the author's full name, the full title of the book, the name of the editor, the place of publication, the name of the publisher, the publication date, and page numbers indicating the location of the quoted information. In subsequent references to the source, give only the author's last name followed by a comma, a shortened version of the title followed by a comma, and the page reference.

Indent the first line of each note five spaces (or one paragraph indent). Begin with a number followed by a period. Leave one space before the first word of the note. If you are double-spacing your manuscript, double-space the notes as well.

Book (first note)

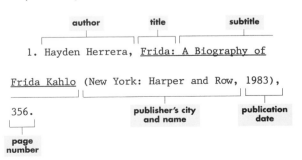

author   title   subtitle

1. Hayden Herrera, Frida: A Biography of

Frida Kahlo (New York: Harper and Row, 1983),

356.   publisher's city and name   publication date

page number

Book (subsequent note)

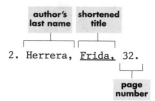

2. Herrera, <u>Frida,</u> 32.

Periodical article (first note)

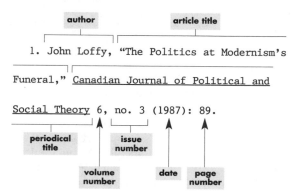

1. John Loffy, "The Politics at Modernism's

Funeral," <u>Canadian Journal of Political and</u>

<u>Social Theory</u> 6, no. 3 (1987): 89.

Periodical article (subsequent note)

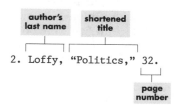

2. Loffy, "Politics," 32.

Here is how you would document the first reference to a source:

▶ According to Professor Tom Wilson, "the idea of the electronic library has emerged as a model for future systems, already implemented in some forms and to some degree in various places."[1]

Here is the corresponding note:

▶ 1. Tom Wilson, "'In the Beginning Was the Word': Social and Economic Factors in Scholarly Electronic Communication," ELVIRA Conference Keynote Paper, 1009, 10 April 1995, <http://www2.shef.ac.uk/infor_studies/lecturer/elvira.html> (23 May 1999), Introduction.

Here is a second reference to the source:

▶ Professor Wilson contends that "a new system of scholarly communication, based on electronic systems and networks, not only necessitates new models for the concepts of journals, library, and publishing, but also new interpersonal and institutional mores, customs, and practices."[2]

Here is the note:

▶ 2. Wilson, "'In the Beginning,'" Introduction.

3 Substitute Internet text divisions for page numbers.

The *Chicago Manual* requires that a note include a page reference or similar information for locating material in a source. Because Internet sources are rarely marked with page numbers, you will not always be able to show exactly where cited material comes from. If a source has internal divisions, use these instead of page numbers in your citation. Be sure to use divisions inherent in the document and not those provided by your browsing software.

In the following example, the Introduction serves as a text division for an Internet source.

▶ As TyAnna Herrington observes, "Nicholas Negroponte's <u>Being Digital</u> provides another welcome not only into an age of technological ubiquity, but into a way of 'being' with technology."[1]

Here is the note:

▶ 1. TyAnna K. Herrington, "Being Is Believing," review of <u>Being Digital,</u> by Nicholas Negroponte, <u>Kairos: A Journal for Teaching Writing in Webbed Environments</u> 1, no. 1 (1996),

---

Box 7.2
Using hypertext to document sources on the Web

The hypertext environment of the World Wide Web doesn't just alter the way you do research, it also lets you document sources in a new way—by using hypertext links. Electronic journals published on the Web are already replacing traditional notes, bibliographies, appendixes, and other supporting text with links to the documents being cited. To read more about hypertext documentation, see Chapter 10 in this book. For an example of how it works, see the sample paper for this chapter (described in 7d), or look at the format of the *Harvard Educational Review* at <http://gseweb.harvard.edu/~hepg/her.html>.

```
<http://english.ttu.edu/kairos/1.1> (24 May
1999), Introduction.
```

7b Notes

See 7a-2 for the basic *Chicago*-style models for documenting printed books and periodicals. For additional information about documenting print sources, see Chapters 15 and 16 of the *Chicago Manual*.

Extending the citation practice of the *Chicago Manual* to include Internet sources produces the following model:

▶ 1. Author's name (in normal order), document title, date of Internet publication, <URL> or other retrieval information (date of access), text division (if applicable).

This model combines the stylistic elements of *Chicago*-style author-date citation[2] with the elements necessary for identifying an Internet source. The publication date appears close to the title of the document, while the date of access follows the **URL** or other access information. The text division occupies the final position in the note, as page numbers would for a printed source.

Internet sources differ in the kinds of information that are important for retrieval, and the model for each type of source reflects the information needed to retrieve that

---

[2]See *Chicago Manual,* sections 15.154 and 15.231.

source. The following models enable you to document Internet sources in a manner consistent with the principles of *Chicago* style.

1 World Wide Web site

To document a file available for viewing and downloading via the World Wide Web, provide the following information:

- Author's name
- Title of document, in quotation marks
- Title of complete work (if relevant), in italics or underlined
- Date of publication or last revision
- URL, in angle brackets
- Date of access, in parentheses

Personal site

▶   1. Joseph Pellegrino, "Homepage," 12 May 1999, <http://www.english.eku.edu/pellegrino /default.htm> (12 June 1999).

Professional site

▶   1. Gail Mortimer, <u>The William Faulkner Society Home Page,</u> 16 September 1999, <http:// www.utep.edu/mortimer/faulkner/mainfaulkner.htm> (1 October 1999).

▶   2. National Association of Investors Corporation, <u>NAIC Online,</u> 29 September 1999, <http://www.better-investing.org> (1 October 1999).

Book

An online book may be the electronic text of part or all of a printed book, or a book-length document available only on the Internet (e.g., a work of **hyperfiction**).

▶   1.   Peter J. Bryant, "The Age of Mammals," in <u>Biodiversity and Conservation,</u> April 1999, <http://darwin.bio.uci.edu/~sustain/bio65 /Titlpage.htm> (11 May 1999).

Article in an electronic journal (ejournal)

▶ 1. Tonya Browning, "Embedded Visuals: Student Design in Web Spaces," <u>Kairos: A Journal for Teachers of Writing in Webbed Environments</u> 3, no. 1 (1997), <http://english.ttu.edu/kairos /2.1/features/browning/index.html> (21 October 1999).

Article in an electronic magazine (ezine)

▶ 1. Nathan Myhrvold, "Confessions of a Cybershaman," <u>Slate,</u> 12 June 1997, <http://www .slate.com/CriticalMass/97-06-12/CriticalMass .asp> (19 October 1997).

Newspaper article

▶ 1. Christopher Wren, "A Body on Mt. Everest, a Mystery Half-Solved," <u>New York Times on the Web,</u> 5 May 1999, <http://search.nytimes.com /search/daily/bin/fastweb?getdoc+site+site+33726 +0+wAAA+%22George%7EMallory%22> (13 May 1999).

Review

▶ 1. Michael Parfit, review of <u>The Climb: Tragic Ambitions on Everest,</u> by Anatoli Boukreev and G. Weston DeWalt, <u>New York Times on the Web,</u> 7 December 1997, <http://search /nytimes.com/books/97/12/07/reviews/971207 .07parfitt.html> (4 October 1999).

Government publication

▶ 1. George Bush, "Principles of Ethical Conduct for Government Officers and Employees," Executive Order 12674, 12 April 1989, pt. 1, <http://www.usoge.gov/exorders/eo12674.html> (30 October 1997).

2 Material from a subscription service

To document an article or other material accessed through a library or institutional subscription service such as EBSCOhost or Lexis-Nexis, provide the following information:

- Publication information for the source
- Name of database, in italics or underlined
- Name of subscription service

- Date of access, in parentheses

▶   1. Robin M. Kowalski, "Whining, griping, and complaining: Positivity in the negativity," <u>Journal of Clinical Psychology</u> 58, no. 9 (2002): 1023. <u>Academic Search Premier,</u> EBSCOhost (19 December 2002).

3 Email message

To document an **email** message, provide the following information:

- Author's name (if known)
- Subject line, in quotation marks
- Date of sending
- Type of communication (personal email, distribution list, office communication)
- Date of access, in parentheses

▶   1. Norman Franke, "SoundApp 2.0.2," 29 April 1996, personal email (3 May 1996).

▶   2. Danny Robinette, "Epiphany Project," 30 April 1999, office communication (29 May 1999).

4 Web discussion forum posting

To document a posting to a **Web discussion forum**, provide the following information:

- Author's name
- Title of posting, in quotation marks
- Date of posting
- URL, in angle brackets
- Date of access, in parentheses

▶   1. Daniel LaLiberte, "HyperNews Instructions," 23 May 1996, <http://union.ncsa.uiuc.edu /HyperNews/get/hypernews/instructions.html> (24 May 1996).

▶   2. Art Saffran, "It's Not That Hard," 5 January 1996, <http://union.ncsa.uiuc.edu/HyperNews /get/hypernews/instructions/90/1/1.html> (24 May 1996).

5 Listserv message

To document a listserv message, provide the following information:

- Author's name (if known)
- Subject line, in quotation marks
- Date of posting
- Listserv address, in angle brackets
- Date of access, in parentheses

▶ 1. Victor Parente, "On Expectations of Class Participation," 27 May 1996, <philosed@sued.syr .edu> (29 May 1996).

▶ 2. Norman Holland, "Re: Colorless Green Ideas," 30 May 1999, <http://web.clas.ufl.edu /ipsa/psyart.htm> (1 June 1999).

6 Newsgroup message

To document information posted in a newsgroup discussion, provide the following information:

- Author's name
- Subject line, in quotation marks
- Date of posting
- Name of newsgroup, in angle brackets
- Date of access, in parentheses

▶ 1. Robert Slade, "UNIX Made Easy," 26 March 1996, <alt.books.reviews> (31 March 1996).

If, after following all the suggestions in 4c-3, you cannot determine the author's name, then use the author's email address, enclosed in angle brackets, as the main entry. When you alphabetize such sources in your Bibliography, treat the first letter of the email address as though it were capitalized.

▶ 2. <lrm583@aol.com> "Thinking of Adoption," 26 May 1996, <alt.adoption> (29 May 1996).

7 Real-time communication

To document a real-time communication, such as those posted in MOOs, MUDs, and IRCs, provide the following information:

- Name of speaker(s) (if known), or name of site
- Title of event (if relevant), in quotation marks
- Date of event
- Type of communication (e.g., group discussion, personal interview), if not indicated elsewhere in entry
- URL (in angle brackets) or other Internet address
- Date of access, in parentheses

▶ 1. LambdaMOO, "Seminar Discussion on Netiquette," 28 May 1996, <telnet://lambda .parc.xerox.edu:8888> (28 May 1996).

▶ 2. Andrew Harnack, "Words," 4 April 1999, group discussion, telnet moo.du.org/port=8888 (5 April 1999).

8 Telnet, FTP, and gopher sites

Telnet site

The most common use of **telnet** is for participation in **real-time communication** (see 7b-6). Although the use of telnet for document retrieval has declined dramatically with increased Web access to texts, numerous archived documents are available only by telnet. To document a telnet site or a file available via telnet, provide the following information:

- Name of author or agency
- Title of document
- Date of publication
- Telnet address in angle brackets, with directions for accessing document
- Date of access, in parentheses

▶ 1. Aquatic Conservation Network, "About the Aquatic Conservation Network," National Capital Freenet, n.d., <telnet://freenet .carleton.ca> login as guest, go acn, press 1 (28 May 1999).

FTP site

To document a file for downloading via **file transfer protocol**, provide the following information:

- Name of author or file

- Title of document
- Size of document (if relevant)
- Date of online publication (if available)
- Any print publication information, italicized or underlined where appropriate
- Complete FTP address
- Date of access, in parentheses

▶   1. everest2.gif [535K], 4 April 1993, <ftp://
ftp.ntua.gr/pub/images/views/sorted.by.type
/Mountains/everest2.gif> (3 June 1999).

▶   2. John Mathews, preface to <u>Numerical Methods
for Mathematics, Science, and Engineering</u> (Upper
Saddle River, NJ: Prentice Hall, 1992), <ftp://
ftp.ntua.gr/pub/netlib/textbook/index.html>
(6 June 1999).

Gopher site

The **gopher** search **protocol** brings text files from all over the world to your computer. Popular in the early 1990s, especially in universities, gopher was a step toward the **World Wide Web**'s **hypertext transfer protocol (HTTP)**. Although the advent of **HTML** documents and their retrieval on the Web has diminished the use of gopher, many documents can still be accessed.

To document material obtained by using gopher, provide the following information:

- Author's name
- Title of document
- Any print publication information, italicized or underlined where appropriate
- Date of online publication
- Gopher address, in angle brackets, with directions for accessing document
- Date of access, in parentheses

▶   1. Jack Goody, "History and Anthropology:
Convergence and Divergence," <u>Bulletin of the
Institute of Ethnology</u> 75, no. 2 (Spring 1993):
n.p., <gopher://gopher.sinica.edu.tw/00/ioe
/eng-bull /75b.txt> (2 June 1999).

7c Bibliography

Since the first note reference to a source includes all the information necessary to verify or retrieve a citation, your *Chicago*-style research paper may not include a Bibliography. If you decide to include one (or are required to do so by an instructor or editor), an alphabetized list of sources will do the trick. (The Bibliography may also be titled Sources Consulted, Works Cited, or Selected Bibliography, if any of those titles more accurately describes the list.)

Bibliography entries differ from first note references in the following ways:

1. Authors' names are inverted.
2. Elements of entries are separated by periods.
3. The first line of each entry is flush with the left margin, and subsequent lines are indented three or four spaces.

If the rest of your manuscript is typed double-spaced, double-space the Bibliography as well.

Compare the following note with the corresponding Bibliography entry:

▶   2. Jason Crawford Teague, "Frames in Action," <u>Kairos: A Journal for Teachers of Writing in Webbed Environments</u> 2, no. 1, August 20, 1998. <http://english.ttu.edu/kairos/2.1> (7 October 1999).

▶   Teague, Jason Crawford. "Frames in Action." <u>Kairos: A Journal for Teachers of Writing in Webbed Environments</u> 2, no. 1, August 20, 1998. <http://english.ttu.edu/kairos/2.1> (7 October 1999).

7d Sample *Chicago*-style hypertext essay

The *Online!* Web site <http://www.bedfordstmartins.com/online> features a sample *Chicago*-style Web essay. Figures 7.1–7.3 show, respectively, the contents page, a sample text page, and part of the Bibliography page of that essay. For more detailed advice on how to compose a hypertext essay, see 9d.

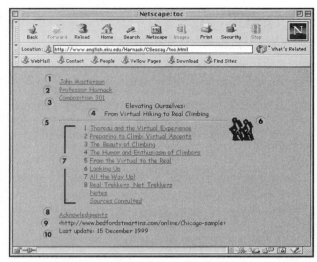

Figure 7.1
Title page of *Chicago*-style hypertext essay

   1   Author's name with *mailto:* link

   2   Instructor's name with link to instructor's homepage

   3   Course name and section number with link to course information

   4   Title and subtitle

   5   Optional use of horizontal line to separate table of contents from title

   6   Optional use of fast-loading image or graphic repeated on subsequent pages to link pages visually

   7   Table of contents with each entry linked to relevant page of essay

   8   Link to optional acknowledgments page

   9   URL

  10   Notice of last update

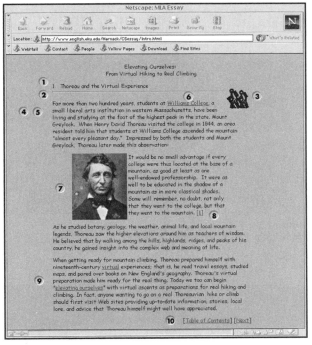

Figure 7.2
Sample page from body of *Chicago*-style hypertext essay

1 Header corresponding to page's title in table of contents

2 Optional use of horizontal rule to separate header from text

3 Optional use of image or graphic

4 Single-spaced text paragraphs of readable length

5 Ample white space around paragraphs and illustrations

6 Hypertext links where appropriate

7 Use of quick-loading images, tables, and/or figures to complement text

8 Links to citation notes

9 Links to content notes

10 Navigation links to table of contents and previous and next pages

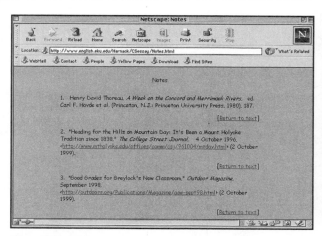

Figure 7.3
Notes page of *Chicago*-style hypertext essay

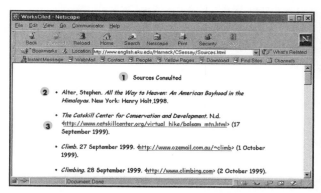

Figure 7.4
Sources Consulted page of *Chicago*-style hypertext essay

1️⃣ Title

2️⃣ Entries formatted as bulleted list

3️⃣ Links to URLs of all online sources

CHAPTER EIGHT

Using CBE Style to Cite and Document Sources

This chapter's guidelines for citing Internet sources stem from the principles presented in the sixth edition of *Scientific Style and Format: The CBE Manual for Authors, Editors, and Publishers,* published by the Council of Biology Editors (now the Council of Science Editors) in 1994. Many writers in the natural sciences use the citation style recommended in the *CBE Manual,* which also gives advice for styling and formatting scientific papers, journals, and books for publication. Its editors offer two methods for citing and documenting sources: the citation-sequence system and the name-year system.

8a   Using CBE in-text citation style

This section briefly describes the citation-sequence and name-year citation systems. Use the system preferred by your instructor or by the journal you are writing for, and consult Chapter 30 of the *CBE Manual,* "Citations and References," for detailed advice. The **Internet** documentation models presented in 8b are compatible with the principles of both systems.

> **Box 8.1**
> **Using italics and underlining in CBE style**
>
> CBE style doesn't specify the use of italics or underlining in References entries, leaving such matters to the discretion of writers and editors. In your writing, you may decide that you need to highlight certain titles, terms, or symbols. The use of underlining to represent italics becomes a problem when you compose texts for online publication. On the World Wide Web, underlining in a document indicates that the underlined word or phrase is an active hypertext link. (All HTML editing programs automatically underline any text linked to another hypertext or Web site.)
>
> When composing Web documents, avoid underlining. Instead, use italics for titles, for emphasis, and for words, letters, and numbers referred to as such. When you write with programs such as email that don't allow italics, type an underscore mark _like this_ before and after text you would otherwise italicize or underline.

1 The citation-sequence system

When using the citation-sequence system, key cited sources to a list of references that are numbered in the order in which they appear in the text. Use a superscript number[1] or a number in parentheses (1) following any reference to a source. (Most instructors prefer superscript numbers to numbers in parentheses. If you're a student, ask your instructor which style he or she prefers.) If a single reference points to more than one source, list the source numbers[1,3,6] in a series. Use a comma (but no following space) to separate two numbers, or numbers[1,3] that do not form a sequence. Use a dash to separate more than two numbers[1-3] that form a sequence. If you cite a source again later in the paper, refer to it by its original number.

In the citation-sequence format, the date of publication is listed after the publisher's name (for books) or after the periodical name (for articles). The following example uses the citation-sequence system.

▶ Ungvarski[1] claims that most HIV-positive patients lose weight as their illness progresses. The World Health Organization has recognized HIV wasting syndrome as an AIDS-defining condition.[2]

HIV wasting is caused partly by an increase in
the level of tumor necrosis factor (TNF). . . .
This increase in TNF leads to the accelerated
muscle breakdown characteristic of HIV wasting
syndrome.[1,3]

Here are the References entries for these three sources:

▶ [1]Ungvarski PJ, Staats J. HIV/AIDS: A guide to
nursing care. 3rd ed. Philadelphia: WB Saunders;
1995. p 47.
[2]World Health Organization. World health statistics annual: 1993. Geneva: World Health Organization; 1994.
[3]Coodley GO, Loveless MO, Merrill TM. The HIV
wasting syndrome: a review. J Acquired Immune
Deficiency Syndromes 1994 July;7(7):681-94.
p 681.

2 The name-year system

When using the name-year system, key cited sources to
an alphabetically arranged list of references. In the name-
year format, the date of publication immediately follows
the author's name. The following example uses the name-
year system.

▶ The discovery in normal cells of genes capable
of causing tumors can be considered a milestone
in cancer research (Stehelin and others 1976).
Recent work (Sarkar, Zhao, and Sarkar 1995) has
confirmed the importance of this finding. As
Bishop and Varmus (1985) point out, numerous
results now suggest that changes in these genes
transform normal cells into cancerous ones.

Here are the References entries for these three sources:

▶ Bishop JM, Varmus HE. 1985. Functions and
origins of retroviral transforming genes.
In: Weiss R, Teich N, Varmus HE, Coffin J,
editors. RNA tumor viruses. Cold Spring Harbor, NY: Cold Spring Harbor Laboratory Press.
p 999-1019.

▶ Sarkar T, Zhao W, Sarkar NH. 1995 Oct. Expression of jun oncogene in rodent and human breast tumors. World Wide Web J Biology 1(1). <http://www.epress.com /w3jbio/wj6.html> Accessed 1996 23 Oct.

▶ Stehelin D, Varmus HE, Bishop JM, Vogt PK. 1976. DNA related to the transforming gene(s) of avian sarcoma viruses is present in normal avian DNA. Nature 260:170-73.

8b References

The *CBE Manual* provides models for documenting electronic journal articles and books, some of which are available on the **World Wide Web** and by **FTP** and **gopher**. The *CBE Manual* includes conventions for citing electronically published articles and books. However, the Council of Science Editors has recently supplemented these guidelines for citing electronically published sources with more detailed recommendations on their Web site at <www.councilscienceeditors.org/pubs_citing_internet .shtml>. The following models enable you to document Internet sources consistent with the principles of the Council of Science Editors' newer guidelines. The examples shown follow the citation-sequence system, but you can easily adapt them to the name-year system.

List the References at the end of your research paper but before any appendixes or explanatory notes. For Internet sources, use the following model:

▶ Author's name (last name, first and any middle initials). Document title [Internet]. Publica-

---

Box 8.2
Using hypertext to document sources on the Web

The hypertext environment of the World Wide Web doesn't just alter the way you do research, it also lets you document sources in a new way—by using hypertext links. Electronic journals published on the Web are already replacing traditional notes, References listings, appendixes, and other supporting text with links to the documents being cited. To read more about hypertext documentation, see Chapter 10 in this book. For an example of how it works, see the sample paper for this chapter (described in 8c), or look at the format of *The World Wide Web Journal of Biology* at <http://epress.com/w3jbio>.

```
tion information. Date of publication and date
cited. <URL> or other retrieval information.
```

Internet sources differ in the kinds of information that are important for retrieval, and the model for each type of source reflects the information needed to retrieve that source. The following models enable you to document Internet sources in a manner consistent with the principles of CBE style.

1 World Wide Web site

To document a file available for viewing and downloading via the **World Wide Web**, provide the following information:

- Author's name
- Title of document
- Title of complete work (if relevant)
- Medium
- Place of publication and name of publisher
- Date of publication, or last revision, and date cited
- URL

Personal site

▶ ¹Joe Pellegrino Home [Internet]. Richmond (KY):
Joe Pellegrino; 1999 May 12 [cited 1999 Nov 7].
Available from: http://www.english.eku.edu
/pellegrino/default.htm

Professional site

▶ ¹[CSE] Council of Science Editors Web Site
[Internet]. Reston (VA): Council of Science
Editors; c2002 [cited 2002 Mar 5]. Available
from: http://www.councilscienceeditors.org

Book

An online book may be the electronic text of part or all of a printed book, or a book-length document available only on the Internet (e.g., a work of **hyperfiction**).

▶ ¹Bryant P. Biodiversity and conservation [Inter-
net]. Irvine (CA): School of Biological Sciences, University of California, Irvine; c2001

```
[cited 2001 Mar 4]. Available from: http://
darwin.bio.uci.edu/~sustain/bio65/index.html
```

Article in an electronic journal (ejournal)

▶ [1]Browning T. Embedded visuals: student design
in Web spaces. Kairos: A Journal for Teachers of
Writing in Webbed Environments [Internet].
1997 [cited 1997 Oct 21];3(1):[about 3 screens].
Available from: http://english.ttu.edu/kairos
/2.1/features/browning/bridge.html

Abstract (in a database)

▶ [1]Isaac JD, Sansone C, Smith JL. IDEAL [Inter-
net]. San Diego (CA): Harcourt; J Experimental
Soc Psychol 1999 May;35:239-65. [cited 1999
Jun 7]. Other people as a source of interest
in an activity [abstract]. Available from:
http://www.europe.idealibrary.com

Article in an electronic magazine (ezine)

▶ [1]Myhrvold N. Confessions of a cybershaman. Slate
[Internet]. 1997 Jun 12 [cited 1997 Oct 19]:
[about 3 screens]. Available from: http://www
.slate.com /CriticalMass/97-06-12/CriticalMass
.asp

▶ [2]Glockle WG, Nonnenmacher TF. A fractional cal-
culus approach to self-similar protein dynamics.
Biophysical J Abstr [Internet]. 1995 [cited
1996 Jul 25];68(1):46. Available from: http://
www.biophysj.org/cgi/content/abstract/68/1/46

Newspaper article

▶ [1]Azar B, Martin S. APA's Council of Representatives endorses new standards for testing, high
school psychology. APA Monitor [Internet]. 1999
Oct [cited 1999 Oct 7]:30(9). [about 4 screens].
Available from: http://www.apa.org/monitor/tools
.html

Government publication

▶ [1]Bush G. Executive order 12674: principles of
ethical conduct for government officers and
employees [Internet]. Washington: Office of
Government Ethics (US); 1989 Apr 12 [cited 2002
```
```

```
Mar 8]. Available from: http://www.usoge.gov
/pages/laws_regs_fedreg_stats/lrfs_files
/exeorders/eo12731.html
```

2 Material from a subscription service

To document an article or other material accessed through a library or institutional subscription service such as EBSCOhost or Lexis-Nexis, provide the following information:

- Publication information for the source
- Database name
- Phrase "database on the Internet," in square brackets
- Place of publication
- Name of subscription service
- Database copyright date
- Date of access, in square brackets
- Number of pages, screens, or lines, in square brackets
- Availability statement with URL and, if provided, the accession number

▶ ```
¹Berger D. The failure of theory: models of
the solar system. National Forum 2001 81(1):
6-9. In: Academic Search Premiere [database
on the Internet]. Birmingham (AL): EBSCOhost;
c 2002-[cited 2002 Sep 28]. [about 65 lines].
Available from: http://web17.epnet.com/citation
.asp?tb=1&_ug=dbs+7+ln+en%2Dus+sid+1DEB684A%2D11
D2%2D4E91%+20010101+dstb=web; Accession No.:
4172628.
```

### 3 Email message

To document an **email** message, provide the following information:

- Author's name
- Subject line
- Type of communication (electronic mail), in square brackets
- Date of sending and date cited
- Length of message
```

▶ [1]Franke N. SoundApp 2.0.2 [Internet]. Message
to: Talvi Laev. 1996 Apr 29 [cited 1996 May 3].
[about 2 screens].

4 Web discussion forum posting

To document a posting to a **Web discussion forum**, provide the following information:

- Author's name
- Title of posting
- Name of discussion forum
- Place of publication and publisher
- Date of posting and date cited
- Length of posting
- URL

▶ [1]LaLiberte D. HyperNews instructions. In:
Instructions for Using HyperNews 1.10 [Inter-
net]. Acton (MA): HyperNews; 1996 May 23 [cited
1996 May 24]. [about 5 paragraphs]. Available
from: http://union.csa.uiuc.edu/HyperNews/get
/hypernews/instructions.html

5 Listserv message

To document a **listserv** message, provide the following
information:

- Author's name
- Subject line
- Name of listserv
- Place of publication and publisher
- Date of posting and date cited
- Length of message
- Listserv address

▶ [1]Parente V. On expectations of class participation. In: PHILOSED [Internet]. Normal (IL):
David Johnathan Blacker; 1996 May 27, 10:17
[cited 1996 May 29]. [about 2 paragraphs].
Available from: philosed@sued.syr.edu

▶ [2]Holland N. Re: colorless green ideas. In:
PSYART [Internet]. Gainesville (FL): Institute
for Psychological Study of the Arts; 1999 May

```
30 [cited 1999 Jun 1]. [about 4 paragraphs].
Available from: http://web.clas.ufl.edu/ipsa
/psyart.htm
```

6 Newsgroup message

To document information posted in a **newsgroup** discussion, provide as much of the following information as possible:

- Author's name
- Subject line
- Name of newsgroup
- Place of publication and publisher
- Date of posting and date cited
- Length of message

▶ [1]Slade R. UNIX made easy. In: alt.books.reviews
  [Internet]. 1996 Mar 26 [cited 1996 Mar 31].
  [about 2 screens].

If, after following all the suggestions in 4c-3, you cannot determine the author's name, then use the author's email address, enclosed in angle brackets, as the main entry.

▶ [2]<lrm583@aol.com> Thinking of adoption. In:
  alt.adoption [Internet]. 1996 May 26 [cited
  1996 May 29]. [about 3 paragraphs].

7 Real-time communication

To document a **real-time communication**, such as those posted in **MOOs**, **MUDs**, and **IRCs**, provide the following information:

- Name of speaker(s) (if known), or name of site
- Title of event (if relevant)
- Type of communication (e.g., group discussion, personal interview), if not indicated elsewhere in entry, in square brackets
- Date of event and date cited
- Length of communication
- URL or other Internet address

▶ [1]LambdaMOO. Seminar discussion on netiquette.
  1996 May 28 [cited 1996 May 28]. [about 3
  screens]. telnet://lambda.parc.xerox.edu:8888

▶ [2]Harnack A. Words. [Group discussion on the Internet]. 1999 Apr 4 [cited 1999 Apr 5]. telnet moo.du.org/port=8888

8 Telnet, FTP, and gopher sites

Telnet site

The most common use of **telnet** is for participation in **real-time communication** (see 8b-6). Although the use of telnet for document retrieval has declined dramatically with increased Web access to texts, numerous archived documents are available only by telnet. To document a telnet site or a file available via telnet, provide the following information:

- Name of author or agency
- Title of database or archive
- Place of publication and publisher
- Date of publication and date cited
- Title of document and its length
- Telnet address, with directions for accessing document

▶ [1]Aquatic Conservation Network. National Capital Freenet [Internet]. n.d. [cited 1999 May 28]. About the Aquatic Conservation Network; [about 2 screens]. Available from: telnet://freenet .carleton.ca login as guest, go acn, press 1.

FTP site

To document a file available for downloading via **file transfer protocol**, provide the following information:

- Name of author or file
- Place of publication and publisher, if available
- Date of online publication (if available) and date cited
- Length of document
- FTP address

▶ [1]everest2.gif [535K]. 1993 Apr 4 [cited 1999 Jun 3]. [about 1 screen]. Available from: ftp://ftp.ntua.gr/pub/images/views/sorted.by .type/Mountains/everest2.gif

▶ [2]Mathews J. Numerical methods for mathematics, science, and engineering. Upper Saddle River

(NJ): Prentice Hall; 1992 [cited 1999 Jun 6].
[about 3 screens]. Available from: ftp://ftp
.ntua.gr/pub/netlib/textbook/index.html

Gopher site

The **gopher** search **protocol** brings text files from all
over the world to your computer. Popular in the early
1990s, especially in universities, gopher was a step
toward the **World Wide Web**'s **hypertext transfer protocol (HTTP)**. Although the advent of **HTML** documents and their retrieval on the Web has diminished the
use of gopher, many documents can still be accessed. To
document information obtained by using the gopher
search protocol, provide the following information:

- Author's name
- Title of database or archive, if appropriate
- Place of publication and publisher
- Date of online publication and date cited
- Title of document and length
- Gopher address, with directions for accessing docu-
  ments

▶ [1]Smith CA. 1994 [cited 1999 May 28]. National
extension model of critical parenting practices;
[about 5 screens]. Available from: gopher://
tinman.mes.umn.edu:4242/11/Other/Other
/NEM_Parent.

8c Sample CBE-style hypertext essay

The *Online!* Web site <http://www.bedfordstmartins
.com/online> features a sample CBE-style Web essay.
Figures 8.1–8.3 show, respectively, the contents page, a
sample text page, and part of the References page of that
essay. For more detailed advice on how to compose a
hypertext essay, see 9d.

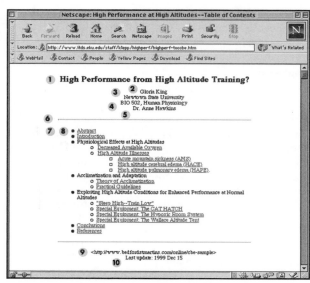

Figure 8.1
Title page of CBE-style hypertext essay

1 Title

2 Author's name

3 Institution's name

4 Course name and section number

5 Instructor's name

6 Optional use of horizontal line to separate table of contents from title

7 Table of contents with each entry linked to relevant page of essay

8 Link to abstract

9 URL

10 Notice of last update

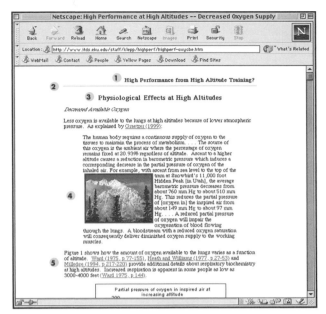

Figure 8.2
Sample page from body of CBE-style hypertext essay

1 Running head

2 Optional use of horizontal rule to separate running head from text

3 Header corresponding to page's title in table of contents

4 Use of quick-loading images, tables, and/or figures to complement text

5 Links to References

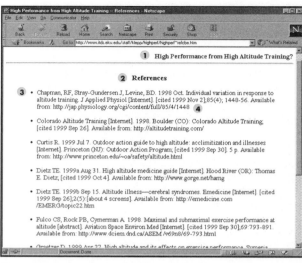

Figure 8.3
References page of CBE-style hypertext essay

1 Running head

2 Title

3 Entries formatted as bulleted list

4 Links to URLs of all online sources

Publishing on the World Wide Web

The **Internet** provides many opportunities for publication—for example, on **listservs** and in **newsgroups** and **Web discussion forums**. Since the **World Wide Web** is the most public, most formal venue for Internet publication, this chapter focuses on the special requirements of publishing on the Web.

Composing Web pages differs in significant ways from writing and publishing in traditional print formats. Unlike printed pages, which present most information in linear fashion, Web texts dramatically expand your opportunities for creative text production and retrieval as well as incorporation of other documents, graphics, sound, and video.

9a Composing Web texts in HTML

You may have occasion to compose **hypertexts** for publication on the Web. A hypertext is a collection of documents containing links that let readers move easily from one document to another. Hypertexts may include graphics, sound, and video, in which case they are often referred to as *hypermedia* or *multimedia* documents.

Hypertexts are created by formatting documents in **HTML**, a code for tagging **ASCII** texts, typefaces, type sizes, colors, graphics, and video to create **hyperlinks**. This formatting is automated by programs such as Microsoft FrontPage, Adobe PageMill, and Netscape Composer. You can also learn to construct and edit HTML code manually, a skill that is invaluable for troubleshooting and improving your Web pages. Here's the HTML text for "Zoo-MOO—MU's Educational MOO Project" at <http://www.missouri.edu/~moo>. Figure 9.1 shows the document as it appears when viewed with a graphic browser.

```
<HTML>
<HEAD>
<TITLE>ZooMOO</TITLE>
</HEAD>
<BODY BGCOLOR="#FFFFFF">
<TR>
<TD><IMG SRC="/moocow.gif" ALT="" HSPACE=5
VSPACE=15 NOSAVE HEIGHT=125 WIDTH=137
ALIGN=LEFT> </TD>
<TD>
<H3>
ZooMOO-MU's Educational MOO Project</H3>
<UL>
<LI>
<A HREF="/history.html">A Brief History of
ZooMOO</A></LI>
<LI>
<A HREF="/zoorequest.html">ZooMOO Character
Request Forms</A></LI>
<LI>
<A HREF="/software.html">Software for connecting
to MOOs</A></LI>
```

```
<LI>
<A HREF="/news.html">What's New on ZooMOO</A></LI>
<LI>
<A HREF="news://news.missouri.edu/mu.comp
.zoomoo"> Read mu.comp.zoomoo (MU campus only)
</A></LI>
<LI>
<A HREF="/resources.html">MOO Resources</A></LI>
<LI>
<A HREF="telnet://moo.missouri.edu:8888/">Telnet
to ZooMOO</A></LI>
</UL>
</TD>
</TR>
</TABLE>
<CENTER>
<H6>
Last updated 2/6/99 by <A HREF="mailto:spif@spif
.com">Bryan Venable</A>.</H6></CENTER>
<center><img src="/poweredby.gif"></center>
</BODY>
</HTML>
```

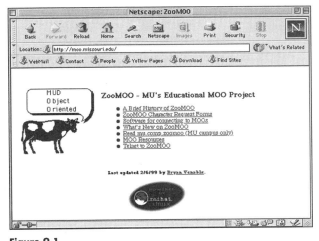

Figure 9.1
An HTML document viewed with a graphic browser
"ZooMOO—MU's Educational MOO Project," 6 Feb. 1999, University of
Missouri–Columbia, 8 Oct. 1999 <http://www.missouri.edu/~moo>.

You can find guides to composing hypertext documents, as well as style manuals for the design of Web documents, in bookstores and on the Web (by searching for *HTML guides*). Here are some of the most popular and useful guides available on the Web:

A Beginner's Guide to HTML
<http://www.ncsa.uiuc.edu/General/Internet/WWW
/HTMLPrimer.html>

An introduction to using HTML and creating files for the Web, with links to additional information.

Learning HTML
<http://www.devry-phx.edu/webresrc/webmstry/learn
.htm>

A resource list for beginning Web designers that includes coverage of writing HTML-based documents.

Composing Good HTML
<http://www.ology.org/tilt/cgh>

Version 2.0.4 addresses stylistic points of HTML composition at both the document and Web levels.

Numerous software programs for creating HTML texts (known as *HTML editors*) are also available. For descriptions and evaluations, consult the following sites:

> *Consummate Winsock List of Basic HTML Editors*
> <http://cws.internet.com/32html.html>

> Web by Design
> <http://www.iupui.edu/~webtrain>

> Webmaster T's World of Design
> <http://www.globalserve.net/~iwb/world>

9b Designing Web pages

Before you start designing Web pages, ask yourself the following questions:

- Who is my audience? What will my audience learn from my Web pages? How will my audience respond when reading my Web pages?

- What are my goals in designing a single Web page or a collection of pages? To inform? To persuade? To entertain?
- How does the content of my Web pages meet my goals?
- Why would somebody visit my Web pages? How do my Web pages differ from other Web pages on a similar topic?

1 Designing individual Web pages

Here are guidelines to keep in mind as you design each Web page:

- *Keep pages short.* Make the text of your document easy to scan by minimizing the need to scroll. It is usually better to create a set of short related pages that each fit on a single screen than one long page. For example, the **homepage** for *Online!* (shown in Figure 9.2) has links to related pages so that you can see at a glance what's available. By presenting all the impor-

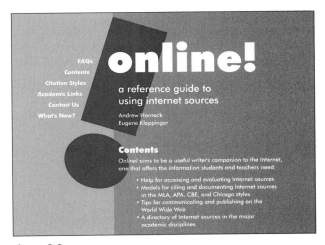

Figure 9.2
The homepage for *Online!*
<http://www.bedfordstmartins.com/online>

tant information up front, this screen allows you to immediately evaluate the Web site's topics.

- *Use appropriate formatting.* Documents created in HTML are reformatted variously by monitors with different-sized screens. Since many viewers use 13-inch monitors, avoid creating Web pages bigger than 640 × 480 **pixels**.

- *Keep paragraphs short.* Since onscreen text is often harder to read than printed text, try not to compose paragraphs that require a lot of scrolling. Whenever possible, use bulleted or numbered lists.

- *Divide long documents into logically sequenced sections.* To help readers follow your presentation of ideas in a document three or more screens long, divide the text into sections. Consider using the conventions of a formal outline (e.g., I, II, III, etc.) with appropriate subsections (A, B, C, etc.) linked to a table of contents. Such divisions not only help readers navigate your text, they also make it easier for them to cite parts of your text accurately when documenting its use as an online source.

- *Use space liberally.* Instead of indenting paragraphs, leave blank lines between them to mark their beginnings and endings. Use space around headings and graphics to create a sense of balance on the Web page.

- *Edit your Web pages.* Spell-check and proofread your Web pages carefully. RxHTMLpro: at <http://www2 .imagiware.com/RxHTMLpro> can perform an automatic check for you.

2 Linking Web pages

It is, of course, possible to publish traditional print texts (conventional essays or research papers, for example) on the Web. Many writers do so. When read on a screen, these texts look like traditional papers, except that they have no page divisions. When printed out, they are nearly indistinguishable from traditional manuscripts. They have obvious beginnings, middle sections, endings, and lists of references.

However, Web texts can also be very different from print texts. Unlike paper texts that follow a fixed order, Web texts can be collections of documents linked togeth-

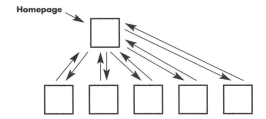

Figure 9.3
Standard linkage
Adapted from Andrew Bryce Shafran and Don Doherty, Creating Your Own Netscape Web Pages *(Indianapolis: Que, 1995) 139.*

er to give readers numerous options. Rather than reading from beginning to end, you might, for example, view sections of a text in a variety of sequences or directions. In general, designers of Web texts rely on one or more of the following basic schemes (shown in Figures 9.3 through 9.6) to link related information:

- *Standard linkage*. In this pattern, you link your homepage to one or more documents, and documents all link directly back to the homepage. (See Figure 9.3.)

- *Waterfall linkage*. In this pattern, you link documents so your readers move from one document to another in a predetermined order. Readers can only go in one direction, as if they were canoeing through a series of small waterfalls. (See Figure 9.4.)

- *Skyscraper linkage*. With this scheme, you link documents so that readers can visit sites placed two (or more) links away from the core collection of texts, but

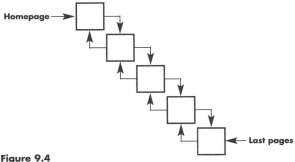

Figure 9.4
Waterfall linkage
Adapted from Andrew Bryce Shafran and Don Doherty, Creating Your Own Netscape Web Pages *(Indianapolis: Que, 1995) 140.*

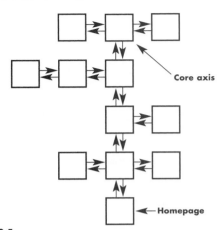

Figure 9.5
Skyscraper linkage
Adapted from Andrew Bryce Shafran and Don Doherty, Creating Your
Own Netscape Web Pages *(Indianapolis: Que, 1995) 140.*

have to go back to the core to access subsequent sets
of links. (See Figure 9.5.)

- *Full Web linkage.* With this arrangement, all your documents are linked to one another so that your readers
  can visit most other documents at most other Web
  locations. This scheme works well when your collection of Web pages is moderate in size. If the collection
  is complex, this scheme may be confusing for readers.
  (See Figure 9.6.)

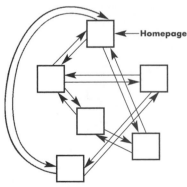

Figure 9.6
Full Web linkage
Adapted from Andrew Bryce Shafran and Don Doherty, Creating Your
Own Netscape Web Pages *(Indianapolis: Que, 1995) 141.*

Many Web writers combine several of these basic patterns, so that their Web document collection may include sections that are standard, waterfall-like, skyscraper-like, and/or fully webbed. How you structure your Web texts depends on your readers' needs and expectations, the kinds of information to be presented, the size of documents, the complexity of relationships among texts, and your use of graphics.

3 Using links effectively

Links let you organize information so that readers can choose what related or supporting material to read. Long definitions and explanations, digressions, illustrations, statistics, notes, bibliographies, and forms to be completed—all these can be linked in separate documents to the main document.

* *Use color to highlight links to other Web sites*. Links are distinguished from regular text by underlining and color. Browsers automatically underline and color links. If you choose link colors other than your browser's default colors, make sure the link colors contrast with your page's background color so that links stand out clearly.

* *Organize links with lists*. Use bulleted or numbered lists, to group related links in logical categories.

  ▶ • Sailing
    • Surfing
    • Kayaking

* *In special instances, indicate the function of the link*. Some links enable readers to send **email**, access **FTP**, or visit **newsgroups**. When creating such links, be sure to make their function or destination obvious.

  Links for sending email. When creating a *mailto:* link, include your name and a mention of email:

  ▶ Email Andrew Harnack
    (in HTML: <a href="mailto:andy.harnack@.eku
    .edu"> Email Andrew Harnack</a>)

  Links for accessing FTP. FTP URLs designate files and directories accessible using the FTP protocol. When creating an FTP link, identify the action with the verb *download:*

▶ <u>Download Psychedelic Screen Saver</u>
(in HTML: `<a href="ftp://ftp.coast.net/pub /Coast/win95/scrsaver/psych20.zip">` Download Psychedelic Screen Saver`</a>`)

Links to newsgroups. When creating a link to a newsgroup's URL, identify the newsgroup by name:

▶ <u>alt.adoption</u>
(in HTML: `<a href="news:alt.adoption">alt .adoption</a>`)

• *Make links obvious and clear within larger texts.* Not all links occur within lists. When embedding a link in a sentence or paragraph, instead of inserting a marker such as *Click here,* simply make the link obvious by color and phrasing. You can assume readers know that underlined, differently colored text indicates a link. The second of the following examples communicates more efficiently than the first example. In the second example, it is obvious that **The Perseus Project** is an active link.

▶ The Perseus Project provides "an evolving digital library on ancient Greece and Rome." For information about the Perseus Project, <u>check here</u>.

▶ <u>The Perseus Project</u> provides "an evolving digital library on ancient Greece and Rome."

• *Take care when using images as links.* When using images as links to other Web pages, use recognizable images so that readers readily understand the linkage. For example, when linking to a favorite song, use an icon that is related to music. When using a **thumbnail** (a miniature image linking to a larger version of the image), consider labeling the thumbnail if the image is hard to see. When using an **image map** (an image with areas that link to other Web documents), make the map and its sections easily understood. If possible, place text in the image to identify linkable sections of the map. For help with image maps, see *NCSA Imagemap Tutorial* at <http://hoohoo.ncsa.uiuc .edu/docs/tutorials/imagemapping.html>.

• *Keep links current.* If you create a link to a Web site that's not your own, check the link periodically to make sure it's still active. "LinkScanQuickCheck" at <http://www.elsop.com/linkscan/quickcheck.html> will give an instant check of links on your page.

9c Creating homepages

Your **homepage** is the HTML document in which you welcome readers to your Web site and steer them to the links and documents available at the site. Personal homepages typically include biographies, graphics, photographs, lists of links, tables, dates of construction and revisions, and the author's email address(es). Business homepages may carry logos, product announcements and reviews, links for contacting corporate representatives, and forms for making online transactions.

If you're affiliated with a college or university, find out whether it enables you to place homepages on the Web. Visit your institution's homepage to acquaint yourself with its policies regarding Web publications by students and faculty and staff members. The homepage may also offer style recommendations and online help as well as links to research sites and to outside sites providing information on coding HTML texts. For a list of policies and guidelines for designing some university Web pages, visit the Web authoring guidelines from selected libraries at UC Irvine's site <http://sun3.lib.uci.edu/~design/othergui.html>.

An excellent way to get ideas for your own homepage is to explore the work of other Web authors. For a look at especially innovative homepage designs, visit these Web sites:

Cool Site of the Day
<http://cool.infi.net>
Presents one attractively designed new site each day.

Personal Pages World Wide
<http://www.utexas.edu/world/personal>
Contains links to collections of personal pages at universities worldwide.

Designing effective homepages
To design effective, readable homepages, follow these guidelines:

* Create an effective title and main heading.
* Use horizontal rules to separate sections.
* Use text highlighting (e.g., italic and bold type) sparingly.

- Use a footer at the bottom of the page for general information (e.g., the site's URL, a *mailto:* connection to the page's owner, the owner's email address), and separate the footer from the body of the text with a horizontal rule.

- Use your institution's or agency's logo where appropriate.

- Use thumbnail images as links to larger images.

- Incorporate text descriptions of images for readers using text-only browsers. (See 9e-3.)

- Give the date when the document was last updated.

Counter shows number of hits   Table of contents indicates scope of site
Footer gives information about page   Rules separate sections

Figure 9.7
Homepage for *Genealogy and History of the Meldrum Family*
This Web page integrates photos, graphics, and text into a succinct, appealing, and informative document. The hotlinks in its table of contents allow readers to delve further into the Meldrum family's background or to explore sites related to the broader topic of genealogy. Ron Meldrum, Genealogy and History of the Meldrum Family, 8 Oct. 1999 <http://www .royalriver.net/meldrum>.

- If the homepage is moved to a new site, leave a notice at the old location directing readers to the new site.

See Figure 9.7 for an example of an inviting homepage.

9d Composing hypertext essays

Composing hypertext essays is similar in many ways to composing essays for print publication. To make your writing clear, well-organized, and persuasive in content and style, you need to use the techniques you would use in any type of writing. Your sentences need to be grammatically and mechanically appropriate. When writing research papers and documented essays, you need to observe all the citation requirements usually associated with such publications.

In some ways, however, composing hypertext essays differs significantly from print composition. The Web offers new possibilities for communicating ideas and information: colorful graphics, background colors, video and sound, and—most important—new opportunities for organizing information. Because the Web consists of linked scrollable documents, it no longer reads—or must be read—like a book or magazine essay. Instead of turning pages or looking at the end of a chapter for notes, you can click on links to access related documents (e.g., a listing of the Works Cited). Section 9b described some ways of organizing hypertext essays. The following guidelines explain how to actually create such an essay.

These guidelines assume that you are using Netscape Composer, a user-friendly **HTML** editor available with Netscape Communicator 4.61 (and later versions). You can download the latest version of Netscape Communicator from <http://home.netscape.com/try/download/index.html>, or you can use another HTML editor and its equivalent functions. As you work, consult the sample hypertext essays at the *Online!* Web site <http://www.bedfordstmartins.com/online>.

Guidelines for composing Web essays

1. As you research your essay, keep careful records of all print and online sources. Record all the information you will need to create accurate citations.

2. Compose the text of your essay in a word-processing program, not in HTML, because word-processed text

is easier to revise, edit, and check for correct spelling. As much as possible, follow the citation and formatting conventions your documentation style requires. Proofread your text carefully before transfering it to an HTML editor.

3. Divide your text into screen-size units and subunits (one to three paragraphs each). You can place a heading at the top of each unit, using a conventional outlining scheme (e.g., I.A, I.A.1, I.A.2, I.B, etc.) where appropriate. In the lower right corner of each unit, write text for a navigation link (e.g., *Table of Contents, Previous, Next*) that will connect the unit to other parts of the essay.

4. Prepare a list of the headings in outline or sequential form to be used as a table of contents.

5. Create text for the first page or homepage that includes the following information:
   • Your name
   • If appropriate, your instructor's name and your course name and section number
   • The title of the essay
   • The table of contents (omit subheadings if they make the contents too long to fit comfortably on one screen)
   • The copyright symbol © and an accompanying notice, if desired
   • The publication date or last date of updating

6. If you are working in Netscape, then, from the Communicator menu at the top of your browser window, select Composer. In Composer, select File, New, and Blank Page. Click on the Table button and create a table with the following settings. (Figure 9.8 shows a table properties dialog box.)

   Number of rows: 1

   Number of columns: 1

   Table alignment: Center

   Border line width: 0 pixels[1]

   Pixel spacing between cells: 0[1]

   Pixel padding within cells: 0[1]

---

[1]Using zero as the setting for border line width, cell spacing, and cell padding allows your text to appear on screen without border lines and cell indications.

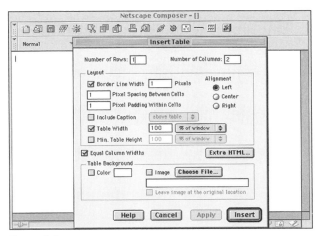

Figure 9.8
A table properties dialog box in Netscape Composer

Table width: 70% of window[2]

Minimum table height: 100% of window

When you've made your selections, click Apply and then OK. A box outline into which you can place text will appear on your screen.

7. Transfer (by copying and pasting) the first-page text from step 5 into the centered single-cell table. Edit the text with toolbar functions (e.g., justification left, center, right) as needed. Create a *mailto:* link from your name to your email address by highlighting your name, clicking the Link button, and entering a *mailto:* expression (e.g., *mailto:gene.kleppinger@eku.edu*). To see how a first page might look, see Figure 5.1.

8. Save the page as an HTML document in an appropriately titled folder (e.g., *sportspaper*) with an appropriate file name (e.g., *homepage.html*). Internet file names must not contain spaces, and names for all HTML documents end with an *.html* or *.htm* **extension**.

9. Repeat the process outlined in steps 6–8 for each unit of your essay.

---

[2]Limiting the table width to 70% makes your text, as displayed, easier to read. Research indicates that text is physically most readable when it has about twelve words per line.

10. Remember to design your pages consistently throughout the essay. Use standard fonts (e.g., Times New Roman) for text. Consider using a small graphic or icon on each page to connect the units (pages) visually. Avoid composing long pages that require extensive scrolling.

11. Follow your style manual's guidelines for headings and other text divisions. On your table-of-contents page, delineate the essay's structure with appropriate headings and subheadings. Use bulleted or numbered lists as needed. If your style calls for underlined headings, use italics instead.

12. Link individual entries in the homepage's table of contents to appropriate files within the folder, using the linking method described in step 7.

13. Link the navigational words (*Table of Contents, Previous, Next*) in each unit to the appropriate files. This linkage allows readers to read the entire essay in order, from the first page (with table of contents) to the list of works cited—or to read it out of order and return to the table of contents at any time.

14. Use links instead of footnotes and endnotes, which many online readers find irritating because their placement at the bottom of texts often requires tedious scrolling. Box 9.1 shows how to create note links in the four major citation styles.

15. Follow your style manual's guidelines for ordering entries on your works-cited, works-consulted, bibliography, or references page. Bullet your entries; don't attempt to create entries in an indented or hanging-indent style. When you need to break URLs, follow the guidelines in 1d-2. For each online source, link the URL to its source document. Don't link the author's name or the title, because the resulting underlining might create confusion.

16. Use graphics and audio and video clips to enhance your text. Add captions to your images by using the Image Properties function (described in 9c-3). If material requires citation, remember to create an appropriate link. For advice on copyright issues, see 3b. For tips on the effective use of images, graphics, video, and sound, see 9e and 9f.

17. Avoid link inflation. If a page uses the word *memetics* ten times, link only one instance to the appropriate source or content note.

Box 9.1
Using hypertext links to create notes

MLA, APA, and CBE (name-year) styles

- For source citations, create links from words, phrases, and parenthetical citations to a Web page listing all the sources. (See the sample essays described in 5c, 6c, and 8c for examples of such linkage.)

- For content and other notes not related to citation, create a separate Web page for each note and link the in-text reference to the appropriate page. (See the sample essays described in 5c, 6c, and 8c for examples.)

Chicago and CBE (citation-sequence) styles

- For source citations, insert bracketed numbers near the cited material (e.g., [1]) and link each number to a Web page listing all the sources. (See the sample essay described in 7d for examples of such linkage.)

- For content and other notes not related to citation, create a separate Web page for each note and link the in-text reference to the appropriate page. (See the sample essay described in 7d for examples.)

18. Test the finished display of your Web essay on a computer other than your own to make sure that all pages are displayed properly and that all links work.

For more on composing Web essays, visit the following sites:

Web Style Guide
<http://info.med.yale.edu/caim/manual/contents.html>

useit.com: Jakob Nielsen's Website
<http://www.useit.com>

Web Workshop
<http://msdn.microsoft.com/workshop>

9e Using images and graphics

The Internet offers a rich treasury of images, icons, graphs, charts, maps, tables, reproductions of paintings, digital photographs, and many other visuals that you can easily **download** and use to illustrate your writing or part of a Web page. This section explains how to find images on the World Wide Web and incorporate them into your work. See 3b for information on how to request permission to use copyrighted sources.

1 Finding images and graphics

With a graphic **browser** , you can visit museums such as the Louvre, view the paintings of Vincent van Gogh and Marcel Duchamp, examine architectural plans in detail, investigate mechanical drawings, peruse weather maps, enjoy film clips of rock concerts, and inspect photographs taken by the Hubble Space Telescope. The following **Web sites** provide collections of background patterns, desktop wallpaper, images, and icons that anyone can download:

Arizona State's Graphics Warehouse
<http://www.eas.asu.edu/~graphics>
Provides background samplers, a color index, and numerous useful graphics such as arrows, balls, buttons, dingbats, and a variety of icons and lines.

The Background Sampler
**<http://www.fciencias.unam.mx/ejemplo/index_bkgr
.html>**
Provides numerous background patterns useful for designing attractive Web pages.

Clip Art.com
<http://www.clip-art.com/>
Gives access to hundreds of free quality clipart images and graphics.

The Icon Browser
<http://www.ibiblio.org/gio/iconbrowser>
Gives access to symbols and miscellaneous icons, plus a search engine.

Netscape: The Background Sampler
**<http://www.netscape.com/assist/net_sites/bg/back
grounds.html>**
Offers a wide range of backgrounds, from raindrops to stucco effects.

WebMuseum Network
<http://metalab.unc.edu/wm>

Gives access to more than 10 million documents containing drawings and paintings from famous museum collections throughout the world.

Yahoo! Computers and Internet: Graphics
<http://www.yahoo.com/Computers_and_Internet/Graphics>

A useful Web page with links to clip art, computer animation, computer-generated graphics, exhibits, and software for holography, morphing, and visualization.

2 Downloading images and graphics

When you use images and graphics in Web page designs, be selective. Because it may take many minutes to **download** a large graphic, good Web-page designers use illustrations only when these deliver information in a way that the text cannot. To help your readers use their browsers efficiently, choose graphics and images that can be transmitted quickly.

The two most common image file formats in use on the Web are **JPEG** (.jpeg or .jpg, pronounced "jay-peg") and **GIF** (.gif, pronounced "jif" or "gif"). Although both formats can be used to include images in **hypertext** documents, they differ in several important ways. On the one hand, JPEG files are superior to GIF files for storing full-color or gray-scale images of "realistic" scenes such as scanned photographs. Any continuous variation in color will be represented more faithfully and in less disk space by JPEG files than by GIF files. On the other hand, GIF files work significantly better with images containing only a few distinct colors, such as line drawings and simple cartoons. For further information and advice, see "JPEG Image Compression FAQ" at <http://www.faqs.org/faqs/jpeg-faq/part1/preamble.html>.

To incorporate into your work graphics you find in other Web documents, first download the graphics to your computer and then create a link. Downloading images, graphics, backgrounds, and icons is generally easy. For example, if you're using the Netscape browser with a Windows operating system, you can download a copy of an image by using Netscape's pop-up menus. First, position your cursor over the image you want to download. Then click on the right mouse button. From the pop-up menu that now appears, choose "Save this image as," and type the appropriate information into the next dialog box . After you enter the information, the image will be downloaded to your computer.

If you're using a Macintosh, follow a similar procedure. Hold down the mouse button for about one second, choose "Save this image as" from the menu, and type the appropriate information into the box that appears. The image will now be quickly transmitted to your computer.

3 Integrating images and graphics with Web documents

When you use images to support textual information, choose visuals that reinforce what you say in your text, so that the visuals help your readers understand your document. Andrea Lunsford and Robert Connors in *The New St. Martin's Handbook* (Boston: Bedford/St. Martin's, 1999, page 657) offer the following tips for using visuals:

- *Use tables* to draw readers' attention to particular numerical information.

- *Use pie charts* to compare a part to the whole. Use *bar charts* and *line graphs* to compare one element with another, to compare elements over time, to demonstrate correlations, and to illustrate frequency.

- *Use drawings or diagrams* to draw attention to dimensions and to details.

- *Use maps* to draw attention to location and to spatial relationships.

- *Use cartoons* to illustrate or emphasize points dramatically or to amuse.

- *Use photographs* to draw attention to a graphic scene (such as devastation following an earthquake) or to depict an object.

In short, base your choices on the purpose of your document and the needs of your audience.

When you use images in a paper or on a Web page, integrate all graphics into your text so that the images and text reinforce each other by observing the following recommendations:

- *Make readability a priority.*

- *Select background patterns that complement the subject matter of the Web page.* For example, many Web-page designers use muted and textured backgrounds that effectively foreground dark-colored textual information.

- *Choose contrasting colors for text and background.*

- *Avoid busy backgrounds.* They are distracting even when contrast is not a problem.

- *Avoid plagiarism.* Use images that are your own, that you have been given permission to use, or that are provided for anyone's use without charge.

- *Keep images as small as possible.* Crop images as closely as possible. Small files load faster and help ensure compatibility with all systems.

- *Be aware of file sizes.* Keep track of your Web page's total file size by adding up the size of your HTML file and all embedded graphics. Try not to exceed 150 kilobytes (KB) for any single complete file, because readers using a 14.4 baud modem will need to spend 1–2 minutes downloading 150KB before they can view the full page. As a rule of thumb, Web pages up to 70KB download quickly and efficiently.

- *Limit individual graphics to 20KB.* Graphics larger than 20KB often take more downloading time than many readers care to spend.

- *Resize large graphics to improve performance.* If your image is larger than 20KB, use a program such as Paint Shop Pro or Adobe Photoshop to reduce its file size. You can let readers access the original by linking the smaller image (a **thumbnail**) to a larger file. Readers can then decide whether to download the larger image.

- *Repeat use of images where possible.* Using the same image in several places helps the browser work faster because once an image is downloaded, it can be accessed quickly from the computer's local memory. It also helps to use standard bullets, bars, and banners.

- *Include text descriptions of images.* Describe images with text for readers who have turned off their browser's graphic display or are using a text-only browser. With an editor such as Netscape Composer, you can add text or captions to your images by using the Image Properties function, which creates text containing a brief description of the image. This information, which appears when readers roll their cursors over the image, reduces the need to label illustrations and figures in the text itself.

For information on how to insert a description of an image into an HTML document, see "Bill Bohan's Introduction to HTML" at <http://one.ctelcom.net/bilbohan/htmltut.html> or the Help screen of your Web-page editor.

- *Provide a copyright notice.* Place the copyright symbol © at the bottom of your page to remind your readers that your material may not be reproduced without your permission.

By following these suggestions for using graphics, you will not only reinforce the content of your Web page but also present screens that are quickly loaded, easily read, and efficiently reproduced.

To find more information about designing Web pages that incorporate images, visit the following sites:

Guide to Web Style
<http://sut1.sut.ac.th/styleguide/printing_version.html>

Evaluating Web Resources
<http://www2.widener.edu/Wolfgram-Memorial-Library/webevaluation/webeval.htm>

Webmonkey: The Web Developer's Resource
<http://hotwired.lycos.com/webmonkey/>

9f Using video and sound

You can add audio and video enhancements to your Web documents. By coding access to small applications ("applets") into an HTML page, you enable browsers to download files containing animation, video clips, and sound effects.

For information on how to request permission to use copyrighted sources, see 3b.

1 Finding audio and video files

Many Internet archives provide collections of sound files in appropriate formats for various platforms. For information on finding and using audio and video files, visit the following sites:

Project Cool Audio Zone
<http://www.projectcool.com/developer/audioz>

Soundfile Information Guide
<http://wings.buffalo.edu/epc/sound/info.html>

You can find specific audio and video files at the following Web sites:

Yahooligans! Downloader
<http://www.yahooligans.com/downloader>

The World Wide Web Virtual Library: Audio
<http://archive.museophile.sbu.ac.uk/audio>

2 Downloading audio and video files

Download audio and video files as you would any file. Once you have downloaded an audio file, you may need to change its format. "Stroud's CWSApps List— Audio Apps" at <http://cws.internet.com/32audio .html> lists and reviews audio-formatting software.

3 Integrating audio and video with Web documents

Including audio and video files on your Web page provides additional ways of communicating with visitors to the page. For example, your page can say "Welcome!" in English or "Bienvenue!" in French; it can display the word *Welcome!* as a rotating sign; it can play a trumpet fanfare as your homepage downloads itself. A musicologist can include sound clips in an essay on Mozart, and film critics can show readers selected scenes from movies under discussion.

While audio and video files can add visual and rhetorical power to Web pages, keep in mind: sound that is appealing to one person can be an annoyance to another, and most video files take a long time to load and require a lot of memory. Be sure that your use of audio and/or video makes a significant contribution to your pages. Avoid filling your pages with gimmicks and features that don't look good or work well together. For help, see "Web Graphics: How to Add Video to Your Site"

at <http://www.builder.com/Graphics/Video/index
.html>

9g Publicizing your Web documents

To make sure that readers find your **homepage** using common Internet **search tools**, you can register it. Since no one registration automatically places your work on the entire **World Wide Web**, choose a registration service that suits your needs and appeals to your intended audiences. Some but not all registration sites charge for this service. To examine sites where you can register your homepage and other publications, visit Meta Search Index at <http://www.mindspring.com/~webgroup/angie/list.html>.

To speed up the registration process, have the following information ready:

- Your document's title
- A brief description of your document
- An accurate transcription of your URL
- A list of keywords that people searching for your site are likely to use
- A list of categories your site would fit into in an index of topics

Once you have registered your homepage, people are likely not only to read your publication but also to correspond with you about it. Reply promptly to any correspondence you receive.

9h Online guides for designing Web pages

The following Web sites offer further information and advice on composing well-designed Web pages and sites:

Art and the Zen of Web Sites (*Tony Karp*)
<http://www.tlc-systems.com/webtips.html>
Simply and elegantly presents advice, truisms, and pointed questions about navigation, design, and technology.

CNET.com
<http://www.builder.com>

A very large collection for beginners and professional designers.

Composing Good HTML (*James Eric Tilton*)
<http://www.ology.org/tilt/cgh>

Discusses Web style at both the document level (describing common errors, giving basic rules of thumb, and illustrating some differences among browser displays) and the site level.

Web Style Sheets
<http://www.w3.org/Style>

Provides links to numerous style sheets and discussions about updates.

A Beginner's Guide to HTML
<http://archive.ncsa.uiuc.edu/General/Internet/WWW /HTMLPrimerAll.html>

Gives thoughtful guidelines for creating Web pages.

Project Cool (*Developer Zone*)
<http://www.devx.com/projectcool/developer>

Provides a set of tools and tutorials and includes numerous reference charts and tables.

The Sevloid Guide to Web Design (*John Cook*)
<http://www.sev.com.au/webzone/design.htm>

A collection of more than 100 tips on every aspect of Web design. The tips are sorted into categories such as page layout, navigation, content, and graphics.

Web Development (*John December*)
<http://www.december.com/web/develop.html>

Discusses Web-page development and describes the characteristics of effective pages.

Web Style Guide (*Patrick Lynch and Sarah Horton*)
<http://info.med.yale.edu/caim/manual/contents.html>

Offers clear, concise advice on creating well-designed and effective Web sites and pages, with expert guidance on issues ranging from planning and organizing, to site design strategies, to individual page design.

Web Mastery
<http://www.hypernews.org/HyperNews/get/www /style.html>

Provides links to numerous style manuals that present, discuss, and debate issues related to Web style.

Succeeding as an Online Student

Learning **online** means that you go to school in a classroom without walls. Without necessarily meeting face-to-face on campus, you and your instructors and classmates share information, discuss ideas, and work collaboratively on the **Internet**. To succeed as an online student, you need to cultivate specific skills. For example, if your course is offered online, your instructor may expect you to collaborate more intensely with classmates and to assume more responsibility as a participant in discussion forums. You may also need to communicate more frequently with your instructor than you might expect to in an on-campus class.

It's a good idea, therefore, to consider your learning habits and attitudes before enrolling in a class that is conducted partly or wholly online. Online learning is likely to be a good choice for you if you have a record of past academic success and can confidently answer "yes" to the following questions:

- Are you motivated to be responsible for your own learning?
- Do you work well independently and within groups?
- Do you follow directions carefully?
- Are you willing to master new computer skills?
- Do you manage your time well?
- Do you know how to find and use resources?
- Are you punctual in meeting deadlines?

If you are unsure whether your learning style matches the expectations of online coursework, consult an instructor or academic advisor who is familiar with your academic record and potential.

If you do decide to give online learning a try, this chapter will show you how you can be successful at it.

10a Understanding what online learning is

Online learning may be defined as education that takes place when teachers and students exchange ideas and information electronically. Although online learners may use print resources such as textbooks, they interact with instructors and other students via **email**, the **World Wide Web**, **real-time communication** (**chats** and **MOO**s), **Web discussion forums**, fax transmissions, telephone conversations, and video conferencing. They may also supplement print resources with information that is stored electronically (e.g., in online databases and on CDs and video- and audiotapes) and in many cases available via the **Internet**. Here are some of the degrees to which your instructors may use online resources:

- Your instructor creates a homepage with his or her contact information and basic information about the course (e.g., a downloadable **syllaweb**, or online syllabus).
- Your instructor supplements the course with material from the Web. The course homepage has links to academic resources, including other Web sites, and you may be asked to acquaint yourself with information available at those links.

- Your instructor richly enhances the course with Internet and Web resources. You are expected to participate in **Web discussion forums** and **real-time communication**, visit and study content-related sites, and transmit files as **email attachments**. To develop the necessary online skills, you may be required to attend an orientation class and/or one or more on-campus workshops.

- The entire course is delivered electronically. Although you may not meet your instructor and classmates face-to-face, you are in frequent contact with them. Your instructor places course materials, assignments, quizzes, and class communications on Web pages. In addition to or instead of a textbook, you may be asked to buy a software program designed specifically for your course of study. After enrolling in the course, you follow the guidelines of a **syllaweb,** master course content, work on assignments (e.g., compose essays, complete research projects, and take quizzes and tests), earn grades, and receive credit for your work—all online.

As schools increase their use of online technologies, you can expect instructors to enhance their courses with more online learning opportunities.

10b Finding information about online courses

Most colleges and universities offer for-credit online courses at the undergraduate and graduate levels. Because it is easiest to register and obtain credit for courses at your own school, start by checking your school's homepage for online course offerings. Figure 10.1 (on page 212) shows the Web page introducing students to online courses at Atlantic Cape Community College. Course catalogs are another good source of information.

If you can't find the online course you want at your school, ask your admissions office, distance learning center, or advisor about the possibility of enrolling for a course elsewhere. Inquire about regional or state-wide organizations that coordinate information, registration, and credit for many colleges and universities. For example, the Oregon Community College Distance Education Consortium <http://www.oregoncollegesonline

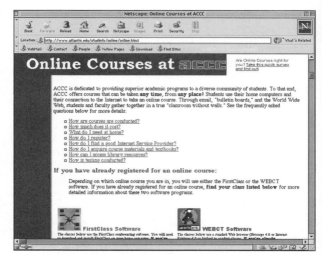

Figure 10.1
**Information about online courses at Atlantic Cape Community
College**
<http://www.atlantic.edu/studinfo/online/online.html>

.org/home.cfm> tracks online courses at about twenty
colleges in Oregon and southwestern Washington.
Numerous other regional and statewide consortia of
schools offer distance-learning courses cooperatively.
Here is a partial list of sites:

Globewide Network Academy
<http://www.gnacademy.org>

The International Distance Learning Course Finder
<http://www.dlcoursefinder.com>

Southern Regional Electronic Campus (SREC)
<http://www.electroniccampus.org>

The World Lecture Hall (WLH)
<http://www.utexas.edu/world/lecture/index.html>.

University of Phoenix
<http://onl.uophx.edu/>

Kentucky Virtual University (KYVU)
<http://www.kyvu.org>

University of Wisconsin Catalog of Distance Learning
<http://www.uwex.edu/disted/catalog>

Lifelong Learning
<http://www.geteducated.com>

Capella University
<http://www.CapellaUniversity.com>

To be sure your school will accept course credits from elsewhere, check with school officials.

Many institutions let students enroll in a variety of noncredit courses without requiring matriculation in a degree program. For example, continuing education departments offer noncredit courses, seminars, and workshops such as "Successful Money Management" and "Internet Basics." To learn more about noncredit courses, visit "Distance Learning: Online Degrees from Bachelor to Masters to Doctoral" at <http://distance learn.about.com/education/distancelearn/mbody .htm>. Not all schools advertising themselves as distance-learning institutions are accredited by regional and national accrediting agencies. If you plan to transfer credit hours from a distance-learning institution, make sure the institution is properly accredited by consulting books such as *International Handbook of Universities,* described at <http://www.grovereference.com/Academic/IHU.htm>, which contains exhaustive current data on more than 5,600 institutions in more than 170 countries, or the Peterson's guide to distance-learning programs at <http://www.petersons.com/dlearn/dlsector.html>.

10c Preparing to take an online course

Once you have chosen the online course(s) you are interested in, take the following steps to give yourself a head start.

1 Getting the right equipment

To get online, many students use the computer facilities at their school's dormitories, libraries, computer center, or student union. Students living in Internet-accessible housing can usually connect their personal computers to the school network. If a school doesn't provide **dial-up access**, students living off-campus will usually need to use an **Internet service provider (ISP)** to secure an

Internet connection. If you are using your own computer, here's the basic equipment you will need to take an online course:

- A computer with a **graphic interface** (Macintosh or Windows)

- A modem (with a speed of 28.8 kilobits per second or higher)

- A connection to an ISP such as America Online, a cable television or telephone company, or a local ISP (found by looking under "Internet" in a telephone directory's business section). Record the telephone number of your ISP in case you need help later.

2 Contacting your instructor

Online instructors appreciate knowing the names, **email addresses**, and telephone numbers of their students in advance so that they can set up courseware and distribute any important announcements. Send your instructor a brief **email** message telling how he or she can contact you. The message can be as simple as this:

```
Dear Dr. Bergen:
I have enrolled in your class JOU 305: Feature
Writing, section 3815.
Donita Fleming
Email: <fleming1479@aol.com>
Phone: 502-891-0000
```

By sending such a message, you show the instructor that you are interested in the course and will take the initiative in learning online.

3 Finding out what software you need

Your instructor may want you to download a program to be used in the course. For example, you may need Adobe Acrobat Reader to let you view and print **PDF** files or a RealAudio **plug-in** to let you hear sound effects. To review the process of downloading programs and files, see 2j.

4 Previewing course materials

You can usually preview the **syllaweb** of an online course by following a link from the school's list of such courses. Look over the syllaweb to make sure you possess the prerequisite skills and that your computer meets the course requirements. Shortly before classes begin, your instructor may provide a list of students' names; a syllaweb; the class schedule; and information about topics such as mailbox functions, announcement boards, discussion forums, lessons, assignments, quizzes and tests, where to store student homepages and Web projects, and getting help with using the course software. (Figure 10.2 shows a typical welcome screen for an online class.) When you visit the course homepage, be sure to **bookmark** it.

At the start of the course, your instructor may give you a **username** and a **password** so you can access and explore the course materials. Write down your username and password and save the information (on paper) in two different places.

5 Learning to send email and attachments

While most online instructors are willing to help you with the basics of online communication, they may expect you to know how to do the following:

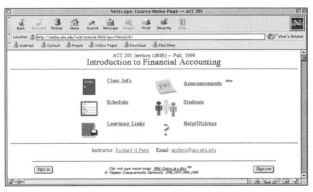

Figure 10.2
Introduction to Financial Accounting
<http://online.eku.edu/Wcb/schools/eku/acc/rfern2/6>

- Use a word processor
- Compose and send email messages
- Save messages for your own records
- Receive and open email attachments

While these skills are not difficult, they may take a little time to master. (See 2c.)

6 Learning to compose Web pages

Some online instructors may expect you to compose a **hypertext** essay or complete some other Web project. For information on how to publish on the Web, see Chapter 9.

7 Learning to transfer files

Your school, your instructor, your **ISP**, or another source (e.g., Geocities at <http://geocities.yahoo.com/home> may provide you with space to store and develop Web pages, graphics, or other files. Moving those files from your computer to another computer may require using **file transfer protocol (FTP)**. For help using FTP, see 2h-1.

10d Communicating with instructors and classmates

In many online courses, much or all of the interaction among students, and between students and instructors, occurs online. Therefore, it's essential that you know how to communicate effectively online.

1 Corresponding online

Email, **listservs**, and **Web discussion forums** provide you with opportunities to communicate with classmates. To stay informed, check your email frequently—daily if necessary. If you maintain several email addresses (perhaps one at school, another at home), be sure your instructor knows which one to use for course-related communication. Your instructor may also use a course-management program within which you can collaborate with individual classmates or the entire class. Always include your name at the bottom of each posting. For information on email, listserv, and discussion forum **netiquette**, see 3c.

If your instructor sets up a listserv for the class, be sure to check postings frequently, read important messages, and respond appropriately. If you have trouble with course materials or assignments, **post** a call for help. By posting publicly, you can open a discussion that others may want to follow. When someone else asks for help, do your best to respond with useful suggestions.

How well you participate in online conversations often becomes an important measure of your success in the course. Listserv and discussion forum conversations are displayed on Web pages as a series of messages arranged in chronological order and/or by topic. Your instructor may create a discussion group for a collaborative project or ask you to participate in a series of class-wide forums. Postings may be dedicated to the discussion of a particular topic, or a single forum may cover multiple topics. Your contributions may range from simple statements of your views to documented essays. Figure 10.3 shows how the threaded messages in a Web-based discussion are displayed.

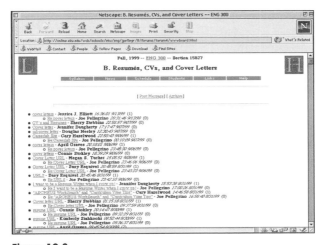

Figure 10.3
A discussion forum showing threaded messages
<http://online.eku.edu/wcb/schools/EKU/eng/jpellegr/8
/forums/forum4/wwwboard.html>

Be aware that many online instructors use computer-generated reports of student participation in forums to help gauge the class's mastery of course content.

2 Using chats

Numerous Web sites such as AOL Instant Messenger <http://aim.aol.com>, Yahoo Chat <http://chat.yahoo.com>, and TalkCity <http://www.talkcity.com> provide opportunities for many people to participate in **Internet relay chat**, more commonly called just *chat*. To "talk" or "chat," participants exchange typed messages. Chats can be ongoing, or they can be scheduled for a particular time and duration. Most chats focus on a particular topic; some involve guest experts or famous people who "talk" to anyone joining the chat. Transcripts of chats can often be stored in an **archive** for later reference. To participate in most chats, you need only register with a distinctive **username** and **password**. Once registered, you select a **channel** or room in which to meet others and enter conversations. Some chat clients (e.g., AOL Instant Messenger) let you select the colors and fonts your words will appear in; they also allow you to record your conversation in HTML, making the transcript ready to **post**. For more information on chats, see 2g and 3c-5.

3 Using MOOs

Your instructor may give you directions on how to go to a **MOO** and participate in **real-time communication**. Like chat rooms, MOOs let many people talk with one another simultaneously. Unlike chats, MOOs provide their users with numerous **virtual** "objects" such as blackboards, lecture notes, and recorders for transcribing conversations. Often built to resemble colleges and universities, MOOs are available for the study of numerous academic topics. More information is available at MUDs, MOOs, and Virtual Worlds <http://coehd.utsa.edu/users/pmcgee/mudsmoos.htm>. Visit <http://www.daedalus.com/net/moolist.html> for a list of the popular educational MOOs.

Participating in a MOO discussion is relatively simple. Your instructor will give you directions for visiting a designated MOO. Although you can participate as a

---

Box 10.1
Basic MOO commands

@who Lets you see who else is logged on. (You type *@who* and see a list of names.)

" Lets you speak to someone. (You type *"Hi. How are you?* and others see on their screen *John says, "Hi. How are you?"*)

: Lets you perform an action. (You type *:smiles* and others see *John smiles.*)

@quit Lets you leave the program. (You type *@quit* and others see *John disconnects.*)

---

guest, your instructor will probably have registered members of your class with *characternames* (**usernames**) and passwords so that you can connect easily. Once at the MOO, you can enter a discussion by first using two or three basic commands. Thereafter, you can quickly learn more MOO commands from the available help menus. Box 10.1 lists a few of the basic commands in use at most MOOs. There are, of course, many more commands; for more information, visit the following sites:

> *MOO Commands and Information*
> <http://www.northern.wvnet.edu/~tdanford /dumoo.html>
>
> *MOO Quick Start*
> <http://www.yeppoon.shs.net.au/student/moo /mooquick.htm>

Many instructors record and email transcripts of MOO conversations to students so that you don't have to take notes on what was said. Moreover, your instructor may ask you to visit your MOO with a group of classmates to collaborate on projects. If you create a log of your group discussion, you can then edit and shape it into a collaboratively created document.

For information on MOO **netiquette**, see 3c-5.

4 Exchanging assignments

When submitting papers to your instructor or to classmates for evaluation, follow the guidelines for World Wide Web and email netiquette in 3c-1 and 3c-2 and the instructions for sending attachments in 2c-2. In addition, remember the following two important points:

- *Don't send a paper in the body of an email message* unless a legitimate technical problem prevents you from sending the paper as an attached file. If you must send a long document in the body of an email message, always warn the recipient first.

- *Keep a paper copy of every assignment you submit*—in addition to the electronic copy stored on your computer—and print out copies of all material you receive (messages, papers, etc.) that you think you might have to refer to later. Do this to guard against the loss of electronically stored data, a mishap that strikes practically every computer user sooner or later.

10e Having your work evaluated

Online instructors sometimes evaluate students' learning with quizzes and tests that automatically score student responses and send the score to both student and instructor. However, online teachers also use many other forms of assessment. For example, instructors may require signs of participation such as a certain frequency of accessing course materials or **posting** to discussion groups. Their course software may provide detailed reports as to how often and with how many words students participate in discussion. Instructors may also examine individual student **postings** and judge them for their cogency, relevance, helpfulness, courtesy, and timeliness. In addition, many instructors evaluate students by examining the quality of larger projects such as **webfolios**—collections of individual and collaborative writing assignments, extended Web essays, or problem-solving projects. Expect your instructor to use a variety of criteria to determine your course grade.

As an online student you will be expected to observe the high standards of academic integrity and honesty typical of serious learning environments. When submitting assignments electronically, be sure your name represents your work. To guarantee the authenticity of your responses on tests, your instructor may ask you to travel to examination sites to take tests under controlled conditions—for example, at other schools, extension centers, high schools, or libraries. You may need to prove your identity before taking a test. To discourage the sharing of answers, some teachers require that students take tests within a limited time window. After an examination, your teacher may schedule a real-time conference to discuss your progress. Remember that online instructors have many opportunities to review your progress and may use a number of criteria to determine your grade.

10f Troubleshooting

One of Murphy's Laws is that whatever can go wrong, will. This statement is particularly true of computers, which most students today use for their coursework. For example, a **server** may be temporarily down, or an **email** message may be returned as "undeliverable." When you encounter such problems, read on-screen error messages carefully. They may suggest that you try visiting the site later, or inform you that you mistyped an **email address** or **URL**. Such information will frequently help you solve the problem yourself—which is what you want to do whenever possible.

If you run into serious trouble—for example, you cannot connect to the Internet or open a file or course software feature—try one or more of the following resources:

- Look for your instructor's **FAQ (frequently asked questions)** document.

- Try your courseware's Help button.

- Many instructors set up forums to discuss difficulties students encounter. If someone hasn't already mentioned a problem similar to yours, post your query. (If, on the other hand, you have solved a problem, post the solution for everyone to see.)

- Ask classmates for help via email. Some of them may have already solved problems similar to yours and may be able to explain and clarify procedures. (When contacting others, follow the netiquette guidelines in 3c.)

- Be specific when reporting your difficulties. If you observe an error message on your screen, copy it down so that you can quote it when seeking help. Rather than sending a message that simply says, "I can't find the Web site," indicate that you have received an error message saying, "404—not found." Someone trying to help you may know that such an error message indicates that the **server** you are contacting can't find the **HTML** document at the URL you've entered. This means you have mistyped the URL, or the document no longer exists, or you've been given the wrong URL. With such knowledge, your helper can respond with specific useful advice.

- Use the telephone. Most colleges and universities maintain a help center staffed by computer technicians who are available for assistance. Your instructor may also provide help by telephone (although you should not contact him or her except during the hours at which he or she has agreed to be available).

If you are still having trouble, consult one of the Web's numerous troubleshooting sites, such as the following:

Troubleshooting Terms Defined
<http://www.md.huji.ac.il/hlpdsk/basics/>
As its title indicates, this site explains basic terminology.

Virtual Computing Guide
<http://www.virtualfreesites.com/compute.html>
Provides numerous links to guidelines and FAQs for a variety of computer problems.

The Internet Help Desk
<http://w3.one.net/~alward>
Offers help to both beginning and advanced Internet users. You'll find expert tools combined with advice on troubleshooting software and connection problems.

Troubleshooting Guide
<http://everythingcomputers.com/troubleg.htm>
A collection of articles that explain the critical issues you need to understand to do effective troubleshooting.

MacFixIt
<http://www.macfixit.com>
Discusses some common problems and how to fix them. These solutions are tailored to Macintosh users, but many apply to other platforms as well.

If you are off-campus and have trouble connecting to the Internet, contact your **Internet service provider (ISP)**.

If possible, visit the ISP's Web site from another computer to see if an **FAQ** is available.

To succeed as an online student, you need to learn the necessary computer skills, take the initiative in locating online courses, communicate well with your instructor and classmates, complete assignments and tests on time, and be ready to solve any problems that arise. For more advice on succeeding as an online student, visit Tidewater Community College's "Strategies for Success" at <http://onlinelearning.tc.cc.va.us/new/n_succes.htm>.

Using Other Styles to Cite and Document Sources

We surveyed style guides currently available in various academic and professional fields and found a wide range of practices for citing electronic sources.

A style manual's publication date often indicates whether the manual is a good source of advice on citing Internet sources. Style manuals published before the mid-1990s (e.g., the *United States Government Printing Office Style Manual*, 1984) make no mention of online sources. Manuals published in the late 1990s (e.g., *The ACS Style Guide*, published by the American Chemical Society in 1997) acknowledge the proliferation of Internet sources, and some provide basic formats and a few models. Many academic and scientific organizations and publications refer writers to other style guides such as *The Chicago Manual of Style* (see Chapter 7) or *Scientific Style and Format: The CBE Manual for Authors, Editors, and Publishers* (see Chapter 8). Others publish online instructions for manuscript preparation, as, for example, does the *Electronic Journal of Geotechnical Engineering* at <http://geotech.civen.okstate.edu/ejge/AuthorsG .htm>. In 1998, Janice R. Walker and Todd Taylor's *The Columbia Guide to Online Style* (published by Columbia University Press) introduced "an interdisciplinary template that can be applied to a variety of already established style guides such as APA, Chicago, and MLA" (1).

In short, information about citing and documenting Internet sources is available, but it varies widely in quality, comprehensiveness, and currency. This appendix gives tips for locating such information. Recognizing that at times you may need to develop your own citation style for a particular situation, we include at the end of the appendix a list of the basic information you should include when citing an Internet source.

If you need to document sources in a style other than MLA, APA, *Chicago,* or CBE, begin by doing the following:

1. Ask your instructor or editor what style, if any, you are required to use for writing in your discipline.
2. Locate the Web site of the organization whose style you intend to use, and look for any guidelines for citation and manuscript preparation.

Following is a list of style manuals, arranged by discipline. A few include advice for documenting Internet sources; others refer readers to their Web sites, or to other sources, for such advice; still others don't mention the topic at all. Consider these sources a starting point. (You may also find leads to style-related information at some of the Web sites listed in Appendix B of this text.)

Biology

Council of Biology Editors. *Scientific Style and Format: The CBE Manual for Authors, Editors, and Publishers.* 6th ed. Cambridge: Cambridge UP, 1994. <http://www.cbe .org>

Chemistry

Dodd, Janet S., ed. *The ACS Style Guide: A Manual for Authors and Editors.* 2nd ed. Washington: Amer. Chemical Soc., 1997. <http://pubs.acs.org>

Engineering

American Society of Civil Engineers. "Authors' Guide to Journals and Practice Periodials." <http://www.pubs .asce.org/authors/index.html>

Institute of Electrical and Electronics Engineers. *IEEE Transactions, Journals, and Letters Information for Authors.* New York: IEEE, 2000. <http://www.ieee.org /organizations/pubs/transactions/information.htm>

English

Gibaldi, Joseph. *MLA Handbook for Writers of Research Papers.* 5th ed. New York: Mod. Lang. Assoc., 1999. <http://www.mla.org>

Geology

Bates, Robert L., Rex Buchanan, and Marla Adkins-Heljeson, eds. *Geowriting: A Guide to Writing, Editing, and Printing in Earth Science.* 5th ed. Alexandria: Amer. Geological Inst., 1995.

Government

Gapner, Diane L., and Diane H. Smith. *The Complete Guide to Citing Government Information Resources: A Manual for Writers and Librarians*. Rev. ed. Bethesda: Congressional Information Service, 1993.

History

The Chicago Manual of Style. 14th ed. Chicago: U of Chicago P, 1993. See also "*The Chicago Manual of Style* FAQ" at <http://www.press.uchicago.edu/Misc /Chicago/cmosfaq.html>.

Humanities—General

See *English; History*.

Journalism

Goldstein, Norm. *Associated Press Stylebook and Libel Manual*. Reading: Addison, 2000.

Law

The Bluebook: A Uniform System of Citation. Comp. editors of *Columbia Law Review* et al. 17th ed. Cambridge: Harvard Law Review, 2000. <http://www.legalbluebook .com>

Good, C. Edward. *Citing and Typing the Law: A Guide to Legal Citation and Style*. 4th ed. Charlottesville: Legal Education, 1997.

Linguistics

Linguistic Society of America. "LSA Style Sheet." Published annually in the December issue of the *LSA Bulletin*.

Mathematics

O'Sean, Arlene, and Antoinette Schleyer. *Mathematics into Type*. Rev. ed. Providence: Amer. Mathematical Soc., 1999. <http://www.ams.org>

Medicine

Iverson, Cheryl, et al. *American Medical Association Manual of Style*. 9th ed. Baltimore: Williams and Wilkins, 1997.

Music

Holoman, D. Kern, ed. *Writing about Music: A Style Sheet from the Editors of Nineteenth-Century Music.* Berkeley: U of California P, 1988.

Wingell, Richard J. *Writing about Music: An Introductory Guide.* 2nd ed. Englewood Cliffs: Prentice Hall, 1996.

See also *History.*

Physical Sciences—General

See *Biology.*

Physics

American Institute of Physics. *AIP Style Manual.* 4th ed. New York: AIP, 1997. (This is an updated printing of an edition originally published in 1990.) <http://www .aip.org>

Political Science

Lane, Michael K. *Style Manual for Political Science.* Rev. ed. Washington: Amer. Political Science Assn., 1993. <http://www.apsanet.org>

Scott, Gregory M., and Stephen M. Garrison. *Political Science Student Writer's Manual.* Englewood Cliffs: Prentice Hall, 1995.

Psychology

American Psychological Association. *Publication Manual of the American Psychological Association.* 5th ed. Washington: APA, 2001. <http://www.apa.org>

Sciences—General

See *Biology.*

Social Sciences—General

See *Psychology.*

Social Work

National Association of Social Workers. Search the NASW Web site <http://www.naswdc.org> for writing advice and style guidelines.

If no guidelines for documenting online sources are available for your discipline, look for advice at one or more of the following Web sites:

Style Manuals and Citation Guides
<http://www.lib.duke.edu/reference/style_manuals
.html>

Internet Citation Guides: Citing Electronic Sources in Research Papers and Bibliographies
<http://www.library.wisc.edu/libraries/Memorial
/citing.htm>

Online Reference Shelf—Citation Guides/Style Manuals
<http://norma.clpccd.cc.ca.us/onlineref/citation.html>

In general, a citation of an Internet source should include at least the following information (the arrangement of which may differ from style to style):

- Name of author or sponsoring organization
- Date of electronic publication or last update notice, if available
- Full title of document
- Description of context (e.g., title of journal, newspaper, or listserv), if relevant
- URL or other Internet address
- Date of access

If you intend to submit work to a specific journal, check the publication's stylistic requirements, which are typically included either in each issue or in the first issue of each volume.

When using a citation style that has yet to provide numerous models of Internet source citations, keep in mind the needs of your readers. No matter what their discipline, readers will appreciate a citation practice that is as simple and consistent as possible and includes adequate information about each source.

A Directory of Internet Sources

This appendix lists URLs that make good starting points for doing research in most academic disciplines and areas of professional specialization.

Because the number of Web sites grows daily, no printed list of URLs is entirely up-to-date. In addition to using this directory, remember to visit the *Online!* Web site at <http://www.bedfordstmartins.com/online>, where the directory is archived and continually updated. Bookmark this Web site so that you can easily visit it.

Sources for the following list include the Argus Clearinghouse at <http://www.clearinghouse.net>, the WWW Virtual Library at <http://vlib.org>, and the 1999 supplement to *Choice: Current Reviews for Academic Libraries.*

a General reference

Blue Web'n Learning Sites Library

<http://www.kn.pacbell.com/wired/bluewebn> links you to a growing number of Internet learning sites (lessons, tutorials, and references), "especially online activities targeted at learners."

INFOMINE: Scholarly Internet Resource Collections

<http://infomine.ucr.edu> offers links to tens of thousands of "academically valuable resources," indexed by subject and educational level.

Refdesk

<http://www.refdesk.com> provides links to search engines, news and weather sites, newspapers, magazines, and reference tools for every conceivable topic, from Acronyms to ZooNet.

Whatis.com

<http://whatis.com> is an online dictionary of Internet terminology.

b   Accounting

ANet Bibliography

<http://www.csu.edu.au/anet/wwwbib/anetbib-welcome.html> is a subject-specific search tool from Charles Sturt University.

AuditNet: Internet Resources for Auditors

<http://www.auditnet.org> aims to be "a complete 'utility' on the World Wide Web for audit-related information, products, and services."

Rutgers Accounting Web

<http://www.rutgers.edu/accounting/raw.html> is the largest accounting Web site on the Internet.

c   Agriculture

INFOMINE: Biological, Agricultural and Medical Sciences

<http://infomine.ucr.edu/search/bioagsearch.phtml> lets you browse or search for resources on all agricultural topics.

Internet Resources for Agriculture

<http://www.aglib.vt.edu/lbmhp/interag.html> is an extensive list of resources cataloged at Virginia Tech.

Internet Resources in Agriculture

<http://www.nal.usda.gov/acq/intscsel.htm> contains hundreds of annotated links "selected by the Acquisitions & Serials Branch of the U.S. Department of Agriculture, National Agricultural Library."

d Anthropology

UCSB Anthropology Web Links

<http://www.anth.ucsb.edu/netinfo.html> is an extensive catalog maintained by the University of California–Santa Barbara.

Voice of the Shuttle: Anthropology Page

<http://vos.ucsb.edu/shuttle/anthro.html> focuses on research-oriented sites.

The WWW Virtual Library: Anthropology

<http://anthrotech.com/resources> includes links to resources for all specialties within anthropology.

e Archaeology

Abzu: Guide to Resources for the Study of the Ancient Near East

<http://www-oi.uchicago.edu/OI/DEPT/RA/ABZU/ABZU.HTML> is "an experimental guide to the rapidly increasing and widely distributed data relevant to the study and public presentation of the Ancient Near East."

ArchNet

<http://archnet.uconn.edu> gives links to news, museums, and academic departments.

Voice of the Shuttle: Archaeology Page

<http://vos.ucsb.edu/shuttle/archaeol.html> emphasizes sites for research.

f Arts (performing and fine arts)

ArtsWire: Online Communication for the Arts

<http://www.artswire.org> tracks news, funding sources, and jobs for artists.

Internet Resources for Music Scholars

<http://www.rism.harvard.edu/MusicLibrary/Internet

Resources.html> is maintained by the Eda Kuhn Loeb Music Library, Harvard University.

Visual & Performing Arts INFOMINE

<http://infomine.ucr.edu/search/artssearch.phtml> is a comprehensive index to Web resources.

World Wide Arts Resources

<http://world-arts-resources.com> "offers the definitive, interactive gateway to all exemplars of qualitative arts information and culture on the Internet."

g   Astronomy

The Astronomy Cafe

<http://itss.raytheon.com/cafe/cafe.html> provides an introduction to astronomy and astronomical research.

The Astronomy Net

<http://www.astronomy.net> offers links for astronomy research, equipment, software, and observatories.

The WWW Virtual Library: Astronomy and Astrophysics & AstroWeb

<http://webhead.com/wwwvl/astronomy> links the major databases for astronomical research.

h   Athletics and sports

[e]ssential Links to Sports Resources on the Internet

<http://www.EL.com/elinks/sports> links you to "professional, college, and general sports information including football, baseball, basketball, and all other sports."

Refdesk—Sports Sites

<http://www.refdesk.com/sports.html> gives more than 100 links to major sports sites and online guides.

The WWW Virtual Library: Sport

<http://www.justwright.com/sports> has an extensive collection of links to informational, commercial, and fee-based resources.

i Biology

BioAgMed INFOMINE

<http://infomine.ucr.edu/cgi-bin/search?bioag>
is a subject-specific search tool especially designed for
research.

Links to the Genetic World

<http://www.ornl.gov/TechResources/Human
_Genome /links.html> is a general index for genetics
resources, with an emphasis on the Human Genome
Project.

Scott's Botanical Links

<http://www.ou.edu/cas/botany-micro/bot-linx> is a
well-annotated index to resources for botany.

Virtual Library: Biosciences

<http://vlib.org/biosciences.html> categorizes
biology resources by type of provider and by subject.

WWW Journal of Biology: Biology on the WWW

<http://www.epress.com/w3jbio/biolinks.htm> pre-
sents a very useful collection of links to major biology
Web servers and webliographies.

i Business and economics

Internet and Marketing

<http://www.ntu.edu.sg/library/mktg/int-mktg
.htm> is a "comprehensive collection of resources to
information on Internet-facilitated advertising and
marketing, Net culture and its relation to business,
promotional sites, statistical and Internet growth information."

BizEc—Select Resources in Business Administration

<http://netec.wustl.edu/BizEc.html> contains links to
selected resources in business administration.

E-Commerce

<http://www.ntu.edu.sg/library/mktg/ecomm.htm>

provides information on electronic commerce, media law, and electronic payment.

Internet Business Library

<http://www.bschool.ukans.edu/intbuslib> has links to news, data, and research reports on domestic and international business and trade.

Madalyn, a Business Research Tool

<http://www.udel.edu/alex/mba/main/netdir2.html> focuses on all aspects of business administration.

WebEc—WWW Resources in Economics

<http://www.helsinki.fi/WebEc> is "an effort to categorize free information in economics on the WWW."

k Chemistry

ChemCenter

<http://www.chemistry.org> is a service of the American Chemical Society.

The Homepage for Chemists

<http://www.chemie.de/~knecht/english/chemeng.php3> provides more than 1,200 links about chemistry.

The WWW Virtual Library: Chemistry

<http://www.chem.ucla.edu/chempointers.html> provides links to Web, gopher, and FTP sites and Usenet newsgroups for all aspects of chemistry.

l Classics

Classics and Mediterranean Archaeology Home Page

<http://rome.classics.lsa.umich.edu/welcome.html> collects sources on topics ranging from ABZU to Xanten.

Classics at Oxford

<http://www.classics.ox.ac.uk/resources.html> features links to classics resources around the globe, as well as ongoing projects at Oxford University.

Internet Resources for Classical Studies and Classical Languages

<http://www.brynmawr.edu/Library/docs/classics.html> is a large collection of links sponsored by the Bryn Mawr College library.

ROMARCH: Roman Art and Archaeology

<http://acad.depauw.edu/romarch/> serves as "the original crossroads for Web resources on the art and archaeology of Italy and the Roman provinces, ca. 1,000 B.C.– A.D. 700."

m   Communications

Kidon Media-Link

<http://www.kidon.com/media-link> offers links to most international media sites, including newspapers, magazines, television, and radio.

News on the Net

<http://www.reporter.org/news> is maintained by Investigative Reporters and Editors, Inc., and has a catalog of Web sites sorted by current media story.

Telecoms Virtual Library

<http://www.analysys.com/vlib>, a section of the WWW Virtual Library, contains a search tool and links categorized by subspecialty.

The WWW Virtual Library: Journalism

<http://209.8.151.142/vlj.html> offers hundreds of links for broadcasting, communications, media, and news.

n   Computing

INFOMINE: Physical Sciences, Engineering, Computing, and Math

<http://infomine.ucr.edu/cgi-bin/search?physic> is a subject-specific search tool designed primarily for research.

PC Webopædia

<http://www.pcwebopaedia.com> offers "accurate, up-to-date information about personal computers."

The WWW Virtual Library: Computing

<http://src.doc.ic.ac.uk/bySubject/Computing/Over view.html> offers links to an online dictionary of computing and to the Internet Computer Index, as well as to thousands of bibliographies and technical reports.

o   Earth sciences

Brock University Earth Science Metasites

<http://www.BrockU.CA/library/research/earthsci /metasite.htm> collects "Web pages that include a comprehensive list of information and links" on earth science topics.

NASA's Global Change Master Directory (GCMD)

<http://gcmd.gsfcnasa.gov> is a comprehensive directory of descriptions of data sets relevant to global change research.

Internet Resources in the Earth Sciences

<http://www.lib.berkeley.edu/EART/EarthLinks.html> offers catalogs of links for earth sciences, planetary sciences, geography, geophysics, seismology, climatology, and oceanography.

The WWW Virtual Library: Earth Sciences

<http://www.geo.ucalgary.ca/VL-EarthSciences.html> is a catalog of resources on all areas of earth science.

p   Education

EdWeb: Exploring Technology and School Reform

<http://edweb.gsn.org> helps you "hunt down online educational resources around the world, learn about trends in education policy and information infrastructure development, examine success stories of computers in the classroom, and much, much more."

NetLearn: Internet Learning Resources Directory

<http://www.rgu.ac.uk/~sim/research/netlearn/callist .htm> is "a directory of resources for learning and teaching Internet skills, including resources for WWW, email, and other formats."

The WWW Virtual Library: Education

<http://www.csu.edu.au/education/library.html> categorizes information sources by subject and permits online searching.

q   English

The English Server at Carnegie-Mellon University

<http:// english-www.hss.cmu.edu> offers links to resources for more than 26,000 texts in many disciplines.

Indispensable Writing Resources

<http:// www.quintcareers.com/writing> helps you "find everything on and off the Net that you could possibly need in writing or researching a paper, including links to all sorts of reference material, links to writing labs, links to Web search engines, and links to writing-related Web sites."

Literary Resources on the Net

<http://andromeda.rutgers.edu/~jlynch/Lit> is a searchable index for English and American literature.

r   Environmental studies

EnviroInfo: Environmental Information Sources

<http:// www.deb.uminho.pt/fontes/enviroinfo> "maintains information on organizations, business, publications, online databases and software, research, and education" for the fields of air pollution, biotechnology, chemistry, ecology, impact and risk assessment, laws, pollution, sustainable development, soil and wetlands, and water and wastewater.

EnviroLink

<http://www.envirolink.org> provides "the most comprehensive, up-to-date environmental resources available."

The WWW Virtual Library: Environment

<http://earthsystems.org/Environment.html> includes links to resources in biodiversity, environmental law, forestry, and landscape architecture.

S   Ethnic studies

Black/African Related Resources

<http://www.sas.upenn.edu/African_Studies/Home_Page/WWW_Links.html> lists information sites concerning black and African people, culture, and issues around the world.

NativeWeb

<http://www.nativeweb.org> collects "resources for indigenous cultures around the world."

The WWW Virtual Library: Migration and Ethnic Relations

<http://www.ercomer.org/wwwvl> is a collection of links to major Internet resources provided by the European Documentation Centre and Observatory on Migration and Ethnic Relations.

T   Gender studies

FMF: Feminist Gateway

<http://www.feminist.org/gateway/1_gatway.html> lists resources on topics such as women's health, women in politics, women and work, feminist arts, and violence against women and is sponsored by the Feminist Majority Foundation.

Gay and Lesbian Politics: WWW and Internet Resources

<http://www.indiana.edu/~glbtpol> is "a selective, annotated guide to the best and most authoritative resources on politics, law, and public policy."

Men's Issues Page

<http://www.vix.com/men> aims "to cover the several men's movements encyclopedically."

U   Geography

The Association of American Geographers

<http://www.aag.org> links you to the work of a

society whose "7,000 members share interests in the theory, methods, and practice of geography."

INFOMINE: Maps and GIS Resources

<http://infomine.ucr.edu/cgi-bin/search?maps> lets you browse or search many map catalogs and libraries.

Colorado University: Resources for Geographers

<http://www.Colorado.edu/geography/virtdept /resources/contents.htm> links you with geographic journals, professional associations, map collections, and other Web resources.

V   Health and medicine

HealthWorld Online

<http://www.healthy.net> includes a medical library, a fitness center, a nutrition center, and a newsroom.

Stayhealthy.com

<http://www.stayhealthy.com> offers "diverse and comprehensive Internet health and wellness resources."

WebMD

<http://www.webmd.com> offers "health news, articles, research reports, condition-specific centers and support communities, interactive tools and programs, as well as online health and lifestyle product catalogues and ordering services."

W   History

Center for History and New Media

<http://chnm.gmu.edu> offers a subject index for history resources on the Internet.

Horus' History Links

<http://www.ucr.edu/h-gig/horuslinks.html> is maintained by the Department of History at University of California–Riverside.

Internet Resources in History

<http://www.tntech.edu/www/acad/hist/resources
.html> is maintained by the Department of History at
Tennessee Technological University.

The WWW-VL History Index

<http://history.cc.ukans.edu/history/VL> categorizes
historical resources primarily by region or country.

X Humanities

LSU Libraries–Subject Guides: Humanities

<http://www.lib.lsu.edu/weblio.html#Humanities>
includes links for all the humanities including architec-
ture, art, classics, film, history, literature, music, philoso-
phy, and theater.

Voice of the Shuttle

<http:// vos.ucsb.edu> weaves together academic,
professional, and scholarly resources for humanities
research.

The WWW Virtual Library: Humanities

<http:// www.hum.gu.se/w3vl> lists resources for
humanities topics.

y International studies

Political Resources on the Net

<http://www.politicalresources.net> lists "political sites
available on the Internet sorted by country, with links to
parties, organizations, governments, media, and more
from all around the world."

Public International Law

<http://www.law.ecel.uwa.edu.au/intlaw> contains
links for all aspects of international law, including the
United Nations and the International Court of Justice.

Worldclass

<http://web.idirect.com/~tiger> gives you "instant
free access and step-by-step commentary for 1,025 top

business sites from 95 countries, chosen based on use-fulness to world commerce, timeliness, ease of use, and presentation."

The WWW Virtual Library: International Affairs Resources

<http://www.etown.edu/vl> categorizes information by area, country, source, and topic.

z Languages

CyberBabel

<http://victorian.fortunecity.com/postmodern/242 /cyberbabel.html> offers links to translation-related Web sites.

EF Education

<http://www.ef.com> lists online language schools and study abroad programs for nine international languages, designed for users from anywhere in the world.

iLoveLanguages

<http://www.ilovelanguages.com> helps you find "online language lessons, translating dictionaries, native literature, translation services, software, language schools, or just a little information on a language you've heard about."

The WWW Virtual Library: Linguistics

<http://www.emich.edu/~linguist/www-vl.html> con-tains links to most of the professional resources on the Web and is maintained by the LINGUIST listserv.

aa Law

ABA Administrative Procedures Database

<http://www.law.fsu.edu/library/admin> is "devel-oped and maintained with the cooperation and support of the American Bar Association's Section of Administra-tive Law and Regulatory Practice and the Florida State University College of Law."

Internet Legal Resource Guide

<http://www.ilrg.com> is designed to be "a comprehensive resource of the information available on the Internet concerning law and the legal profession, with an emphasis on the United States of America."

Law Library Resource Xchange

<http://www.llrx.com/sources.html> contains a thorough index for all types of legal information.

bb Libraries and information science

Library and Information Science

<http://www.lub.lu.se/netlab/documents/lisres.html> is "a comprehensive Web database designed to provide a one-stop shopping center for librarians to locate Internet resources related to their profession."

Library and Information Science

<http://www.lub.lu.se/netlab/documents/lisres.html> is an extensive collection of annotated links and search strategies.

LibraryLand

<http://sunsite.berkeley.edu/LibraryLand> is a subject guide for all librarianship topics.

PICK

<http://www.aber.ac.uk/~tplwww/e/pick.html> is "a gateway to quality library and information science (aka LIS or librarianship) resources on the Internet."

cc Literature

Internet Book Information Center

<http://www.internetbookinfo.com> "represents a massive, somewhat obsessive attempt, written primarily (but not exclusively) by a single individual, to provide comprehensive coverage of a very wide range of issues and interests in the field of books."

Literary Resources on the Net

<http://andromeda.rutgers.edu/~jlynch/Lit> provides access to Web sites for literature in all periods, ancient to contemporary.

Literature and Composition Resources

<http://www.frostburg.edu/dept/engl/gartner /Litcomp.htm> seeks to identify high-quality primary and secondary sources for students and teachers.

Malaspina Great Books Home Page

<http://www.mala.bc.ca/~mcneil/template.htx> covers links for Web resources about the Great Books series.

dd Mathematics

A Catalog of Mathematics Resources

<http://mthwww.uwc.edu/wwwmahes/files/math01 .html> is an extensive compilation of links to U.S. and international math sites.

Math Forum Internet Mathematics Library

<http://forum.swarthmore.edu/library> is an annotated catalog of links for all mathematics topics.

Statistics-Related Internet Sources

<http://www.dartmouth.edu/~chance/RelatedSources /sources.html>, part of the Chance Database project, is an annotated catalog.

The WWW Virtual Library: Mathematics

<http://euclid.math.fsu.edu/Science/math.html> has links for research and education in all areas of mathematics.

ee Nursing

Nursing

<http://www.atnursing.com> is a search engine specializing in topics for nursing and health.

NursingNet

<http://www.nursingnet.org> is designed to "further the knowledge and understanding of nursing for the public, and to provide a forum for medical professionals and students to obtain and disseminate information about nursing and medically related subjects."

ff   Philosophy

Hippias: Limited Area Search of Philosophy on the Internet

<http://hippias.evansville.edu> is a search tool for philosophy resources.

Philosophy in Cyberspace

<http://www-personal.monash.edu.au/~dey/phil> is an annotated guide to thousands of philosophy-related resources on the Internet.

Religion and Philosophy Resources on the Internet

<http://www.bu.edu/sth/library/resources.html> "provides a selected listing of local and worldwide Internet sources for religion and philosophy," with brief annotations for each item.

The WWW Virtual Library: Philosophy

<http://www.bris.ac.uk/Depts/Philosophy/VL> offers links to resources on all aspects of philosophy and to many other detailed guides.

gg   Physics

INFOMINE: Physical Sciences, Engineering, Computing, and Math

<http://infomine.ucr.edu/cgi-bin/search?physci> offers a subject index for physics resources.

PhysLINK.com

<http://www.physlink.com> covers resources in physics, science, and engineering, with links to an extensive collection of reference works.

TIPTOP: The Internet Pilot to Physics

<http://physics.hallym.ac.kr/education/TIPTOP> lists thousands of physics resources and features "the world's most comprehensive index to online physics resources."

The WWW Virtual Library: Physics

<http://www.vlib.org/Physics.html> categorizes physics resources by topic and by specialized field.

hh Political science

International Relations and Security Network

<http://www.isn.ethz.ch> holds the International Security section of the WWW Virtual Library and offers links to current political data and educational ventures.

Political Science Resources on the Web

<http://www.lib.umich.edu/libhome/Documents .center/polisci.html> indexes resources for teachers, students, and researchers on all aspects of political science.

Richard Kimber's Political Science Resources

<http://www.psr.keele.ac.uk> provides links to material about current elections, national constitutions, political theory and thought, and government data at the national and local levels.

ii Psychology

Mental Help Net

<http://mentalhelp.net> is an extensive guide to resources for mental health, psychology, and psychiatry.

PsychWeb

<http://www.psywww.com>, part of the Psych Web project, links you to sites on all aspects of psychology.

Social Psychology Network

<http://www.socialpsychology.org> is "the social psychology database on the Internet."

The WWW Virtual Library: Psychology

<http://www.clas.ufl.edu/users/gthursby/psi> has links for all branches of psychology.

jj Sociology

SocioSite

<http://www.pscw.uva.nl/sociosite> includes "high-quality resources and texts from all sociological fields, from all countries, and in any language."

The SocioWeb

<http://www.socioweb.com/~markbl/socioweb> has links to sociological resources and a subject-specific index.

The WWW Virtual Library: Sociology

<http://www.mcmaster.ca/socscidocs/w3virtsoclib /index.htm> collects resources on all aspects of sociology.

kk Special needs

Blindness Resource Center

<http://www.nyise.org/blind.htm> is maintained by The New York Institute for Special Education.

Indie: Integrated Network of Disability Information and Education

<http://laurence.canlearn.ca/indie> is a comprehensive site for people with disabilities worldwide.

Kids Together

<http://www.kidstogether.org> has information and resources for children and adults with disabilities.

ll Technology and applied arts

Edinburgh Engineering Virtual Library

<http://www.eevl.ac.uk/welcome.html> has an extensive database of engineering resources with browsing and searching tools.

ICE: Internet Connections for Engineering

<http://www.englib.cornell.edu/ice> provides "a broad catalog of Internet-based engineering resources to allow engineers, researchers, engineering students, and faculty to find useful information."

Engineering Resources Online

<http://www.er-online.co.uk> offers links to resources on all aspects of engineering.

mm Theater

McCoy's Guide to Theatre and Performance Studies

<http://www.stetson.edu/departments/csata/thr_guid .html> is an extensive, annotated list for all theatrical and performance topics.

Playbill Online Presents Theatre Central

<http://www1.playbill.com/cgi-bin/plb/central?cmd =start> is "the largest compendium of theatre links on the Internet."

World Wide Arts Resources: Theater

<http://wwar.com/categories/Theater> "will lead you to thousands of theater-related resources."

WWW Virtual Library: Theatre and Drama

<http://vl-theatre.com> offers links "for professionals, amateurs, academics and students of all ages."

nn Writing

Grammar, Usage and Style

<http://www.refdesk.com/factgram.html> offers hundreds of annotated links to resources for editing all forms of written communication.

Inkspot: Writing-Related Resources

<http://www.inkspot.com> "offers over 2,000 pages of information about the craft and business of writing, as well as dozens of discussion forums and other online networking opportunities."

Online Resources for Writers

<http://webster.commnet.edu/writing/writing.htm>
features links to online reference tools, ezines, and grammar and style sites.

Web Resources for Writers

<http://www.bedfordstmartins.com/lunsford/weblinks/toc.htm> has links to general reference tools and sites specifically aimed at helping teachers and all writers.

Acknowledgments

(*continued from copyright page*)

INFOMINE homepage and query results screen shots, from http://infomine.ucr.edu. Copyright © 2003 The Regents of the University of California. Reprinted by permission of INFOMINE.

The Meldrum Family Web page. Reprinted with permission.

Microsoft Homepage screen. Copyright © 1999 Microsoft Corporation. Reprinted with permission from Microsoft Corporation.

Netscape screens. Copyright © 1999 Netscape Communications Corp. Used with permission. All Rights Reserved. This electronic file or page may not be reprinted or copied without the express written permission of Netscape.

Netscape Communications Corporation has not authorized, sponsored, or endorsed, or approved this publication and is not responsible for its content. Netscape and the Netscape Communications Corporate Logos are trademarks and trade names of Netscape Communications Corporation. All other product names and/or logos are trademarks of their respective owners.

Project Gutenberg Web Site. Copyright © 1971–1998 Project Gutenberg and Promo.net.

PROMO.NET. All Rights Reserved. Web site designed and administered by Pietro Di Miceli, webmaster of Promonet. The Original URL of Project Gutenberg Web site is: http//promo.net. Reprinted by permission.

Andrew Bryce Shafran and Don Doherty. Figures 9.3–9.6 adapted from *Creating Your Own Netscape Web Pages* by Andrew Bryce Shafran and Don Doherty. Copyright 1995 by Que Corporation. Reprinted with the permission of Que, an imprint of Macmillan USA, a division of Pearson Education.

Whatis?com screens. Copyright © 1996–1999 Whatis.com, Inc. All Rights Reserved. Used with permission.

YAHOO! Screens. Text and artwork copyright © 1999 by Yahoo! Inc. All Rights Reserved. YAHOO! And the YAHOO! Logo are trademarks of YAHOO! Inc. Used with permission.

Zion National Park Chat Page. The Watchman–Coral © Copyright. By John William Uhler. Copyright © 1997–1999 Page-Makers, L.L.C. Reproduced by permission.

Index